The Powow River Poets Anthology II

The
POWOW RIVER POETS

ANTHOLOGY II

EDITED BY *Paulette Demers Turco*

INTRODUCTION BY *Leslie Monsour*

ABLE MUSE PRESS

Able Muse Press

www.ablemusepress.com

Library of Congress Cataloging-in-Publication Data

Names: Turco, Paulette Demers, 1950- editor. | Monsour, Leslie, writer of introduction.
Title: The Powow River Poets Anthology II / edited by Paulette Demers Turco ; introduction by Leslie Monsour.
Description: San Jose, CA : Able Muse Press, 2020.
Identifiers: LCCN 2020022057 (print) | LCCN 2020022058 (ebook) | ISBN 9781773490755 (paperback) | ISBN 9781773490762 (ebook)
Subjects: LCSH: American poetry.
Classification: LCC PS586 .P68 2020 (print) | LCC PS586 (ebook) | DDC 811/.608--dc23
LC record available at https://lccn.loc.gov/2020022057
LC ebook record available at https://lccn.loc.gov/2020022058

Printed in the United States of America

Cover image: *Plant & Water* by Alexander Pepple
          (with *Creativity* by cdd20 and *Water* by George Athens)

Cover & book design by Alexander Pepple

Poems previously published by Finishing Line Press are reprinted by permission of the Permissions Company LLC on behalf of Finishing Line Press, finishinglinepress.com.

Paulette Demers Turco photo (page 136) by Greg Nikas Photography

Able Muse Press is an imprint of *Able Muse:* A Review of Poetry, Prose & Art—at www.ablemuse.com

Able Muse Press
467 Saratoga Avenue #602
San Jose, CA 95129

With thanks

to the accomplished poets
Rhina P. Espaillat, Alfred Nicol, and Jean L. Kreiling,
who served as readers and advisors
in the making of this anthology

and to the Newburyport Public Library
for providing us a place to gather every month
to share our work.

★

The Powow River Poets are a gathering of widely published, award-winning New England poets, centered in Newburyport, Massachusetts, but including members from the Boston area and from as far away as New York and Maine. This collection is their sequel to *The Powow River Anthology* (Ocean Publishing, 2006), edited by Alfred Nicol, with an introduction by X.J. Kennedy. More about the Powow River Poets can be found at powowriverpoets.com.

Introduction

"Steer toward the music . . ."

I T MIGHT BE far-fetched to suggest that the Muses have sprinkled a generous share of their gifts into the waters of the Powow River as it pours out of Lake Gardner into the Merrimack and flows east to the Atlantic Ocean at the historic town of Newburyport on the northern coast of Massachusetts, where the Powow River Poets established their home base three decades ago—but how else to explain the lyric fluency, robust talent, and refreshing wit that consistently distinguish this group?

In his introduction to the first Powow River anthology in 2006, X.J. Kennedy came up with a more down-to-earth explanation when he wrote that the group's success "has sprung from a nourishing environment, human contacts, and plenty of good-natured argument over how a line ought to stand." Kennedy is right, of course; but something else has made this group extra special all these years, and it might have something to do with the cofounder Rhina P. Espaillat, a poetry magnet, who consistently attracts playful camaraderie and human warmth while maintaining a disciplined dedication to her art.

Let's take a look at what might *not* have happened by eliminating certain links in the chain of events that led Espaillat to Newburyport: had she *not* been born in the Dominican Republic in 1932; had she *not* been forced to flee her country's brutal dictatorship; had her family *not* been granted asylum in the US; had they *not* settled in New York City; had Espaillat, through her family and her schooling, *not* developed a strong love for language, for poetry, and for people; had she *not* married Alfred Moskowitz, a teacher and a sculptor; had she and Moskowitz *not* raised two sons who went to MIT; had her two sons *not* found positions as physicists in the Newburyport area; had Espaillat's mother *not* fallen victim to the sorrows and cruelties of Alzheimer's disease; had Espaillat and her husband *not* visited their sons and discovered Newburyport's superior residential facility for Alzheimer's patients, as well as an affordable neighborhood nearby— then, it's safe to say they would *not* have moved to Newburyport in 1990, Espaillat would *not* have promptly set about attracting all the poets within range, who would *not* have begun holding workshops in each other's homes, and the Powow River Poets would almost certainly *not* be what they are today.

By the time their first anthology came out, several of the poets had already published award-winning books. Fourteen years later, almost half have stayed on to be included in the second anthology, and several more of them have turned in award-winning manuscripts. Meanwhile, the group has been replenished and expanded with more "newcomers," many of them prizewinning, seasoned poets as well, who have gravitated to the workshop, principally from various parts of Massachusetts, but also from Maine, New Hampshire, Connecticut, even New York. As a Californian, I've always marveled at and envied the geographic proximity and ease of travel that exists in the northeastern states, which can only help a group like this maintain its quality and longevity.

The new anthology is dedicated to one of the group's longtime members, David Berman, who passed away in 2017. The dedication includes his poem "The Effect of Hearing the Sublime" and entreats us, in the voice of Odysseus, to "steer toward the music." The hero's men can't hear him but we can, as we sail irresistibly toward the musicality of the well-made metrical verse collected here. Like its predecessor, the new anthology offers a banquet of sonnets and other stanzaic forms, including terza rima, villanelle, triolet, heroic couplet, blank verse narrative, and one virtuoso sestina by Paulette Demers Turco.

Formal verse has always been favored in this group; but skillfully rendered free verse is never excluded, as Wendy Cannella's fascinating ekphrastic poem "Message from a Dead Pearl Diver" and her edifying treatise on "The Word *Slut*" aptly demonstrate. Midge Goldberg also slips in a couple of free verse poems along with her sonnets and quatrains, marking a rare fluid ease in both open form and metrical verse, as do Kyle Potvin, Joan Alice Wood Kimball, and even A.M. Juster (albeit as a joke: more later).

What these poets require of themselves are poems that are made to be understood. Robert Frost, who famously lived *North of Boston* and whose work is well known to members of this group, also shared the desire to be understood adding with characteristic mischief, "to a point." Frost's influence is detectable in several of the poems here.

In Robert W. Crawford's "Hawks in the Leaves," for instance, the air shivers with Frostian edginess. Crawford, Poet Laureate of Derry, New Hampshire, and Director of the Frost Farm Poetry Conference, keeps chickens, as Frost did. He conjures a particular New England spookiness when he communes with his hens in the stillness of an autumn day and senses an eeriness in the atmosphere: "And so the hens and I believe there's more / to this world than meets the casual eye. A whiff / of woodsmoke and the closing of a door; / I don't know all that's happening here. . . ." In another instance, the chilling effect of Frost's narrative poem "Out, Out" permeates Crawford's "Grappling Hook," which also deals with the matter-of-fact retelling of a youth's accidental death. Meredith Bergmann's "From the New House," in which she comes across the exposed bones of an unidentifiable creature half-buried in the frozen soil, like a skeleton that escaped from some old closet, made me think of "the bones. . . . The cellar bones—out of the grave" from Frost's petrifying masterpiece "The Witch of Coös."

As well as the chill factor, Robert Frost had plenty of warmth to share. There's a gleam of "The Road Not Taken" in David Davis's poem "The Waterfall" when he escapes from his cubicle workspace to hike "a trail I chose at random from a map. / Passed once too often by a mountain bike, / I left the path and climbed the ridge. . . ." Davis opts out of one route and takes the other only to discover a waterfall hidden in the rocks, and that made all the difference.

Water is plentiful in the natural environment of the New England countryside. Its lakes, ponds, streams, brooks, and coastlines appear throughout these pages. Alfred Nicol's handsomely made sestets in "At Dusk" describe October on Plum Island, where Newburyport meets the Atlantic. Nicol and a friend "sit on a ridge of sand" watching the changing light as "Slowly, now, a darkness fills the hollows" and "Splotches of sunset founder in the rills." The momentary effect of day turning into night is not unlike a semiconscious dream and when Nicol's friend says she is dreaming of guava trees in La Vega, we can safely guess that Rhina P. Espaillat is the friend sitting next to him.

Espaillat takes us to the riverfront in "On the Promenade" for a bittersweet moment of humor with her mother, "Widowed, confused, dimly aware / of who I was beside her there, / but fond of mischief and still pretty. / She loved the river and the city, // seagulls and sailboats skimming by." The two of them are taking their habitual stroll on the boardwalk along "the sun-speckled Merrimack," when they are joined by an old fellow with a cane. Espaillat suggests to her mother that the gentleman is smitten. Her mother's lucid, decisive rebuff is a self-assured, woman-to-woman moment to enjoy.

Everything about life near the water changes when winter comes to this part of the country. The icy climate penetrates more than meets the eye in Jean L. Kreiling's "Winter Boats," when she interprets the ambience with an accuracy no picture could capture, observing how "Becalmed in backyards, cold and mortified, / boats hold their breath. . . ." Likewise, Midge Goldberg leads us right onto a frozen lake in "Walking on Ice," where "The fishermen are out without a boat," and "The only ones unsure out here are geese, / who clamor cautiously onto the lake." Toni Treadway's "Late Harvest" of "berries that withstand the frost" with "liquored juice and puckered flesh" is rich with a sensual intensity one doesn't expect to find in a frozen garden.

In a warmer garden, Deborah Warren considers the mole, casting him as a "geonaut supreme," invisible but audible "an inch beneath my sole." When she pictures her own "habitat of thought" well above ground in her "windy lair" like "an animal who can dig a hole in air," she conjures the star-nosed moles that fly in the heavens and the sparrows that burrow in the sky from "Praise in Summer" by Richard Wilbur, who lived and taught in Massachusetts most of his life and whose work is cherished and honored by the Powow River Poets.

I can probably speak for many longtime Californians when I say that when I visit New England from the West Coast, I feel as though I've gone back in time two or three centuries to the days of the American Revolution; and, when I leave America to visit my Olde English roots across the Atlantic, I feel as though I've gone back a thousand years more. However, in "Genealogy," James Najarian telescopes in time from 1968 all the way back to the singularity of the uncreated universe by staying put on two hundred acres of Pennsylvania farmland. "The Informant" by Anton Yakovlev takes us time-traveling in a story of heredity with a complicated tale of cold-blooded politics and power, disguised as a simple ballad. In "Shards of Knowing," Barbara Lydecker Crane travels to the past in the modern Czech Republic by taking a tour of man's inhumanity to man in what remains of a Soviet labor camp. We find ourselves in the midst of our own contemporary history in Rhina P. Espaillat's poem "Bra" that begins, "What a good fit! But the label says Honduras," and goes on to stir our collective conscience and nostalgia for the days when labels on women's clothing were stamped with the ILGWU emblem (International Ladies' Garment Workers' Union). Alas, no more. So much has been lost in such a short time, we can only sigh, as Espaillat does, "How burdened every choice is with politics, guilt. . . ." In another instance of current history, José Edmundo Ocampo Reyes addresses the perils of immigration with "Instructions to Travelers from the Third World," as he examines the concept of the passport and explains to the migrant, "Your photo may adorn it, but it really is the property of your crumbling republic, / as you are."

Earlier I compared this anthology to a banquet, so be sure to save room for dessert. A healthy balance of refreshing wit is on the menu. Don't skip M. Frost Delaney's "What Joseph Might Have Said." It made me laugh out loud and immediately want to share it with family and friends. It's perfect for the holidays, but I couldn't wait that long. In a darker shade of mirth, Alfred Nicol's childhood memory "October 1962" tells of the Cuban missile crisis and his mother's endearing giddiness, as she goes about preparing her children for nuclear holocaust. You won't want to miss A.M. Juster's "Proposed Clichés," and, after you finally stop laughing at "Love Song," Juster's parody of a certain former Poet Laureate, you'll want to go back for seconds, but to do so you'll have to seek out Juster's 2016 collection, *The Billy Collins Experience.*

If all this is beginning to sound like a colorful dinner party with a group of delightfully memorable guests, pull up a chair and feast your heart and mind on the flavorful and nourishing dishes served within these pages.

Buen provecho.

Leslie Monsour
Los Angeles, California
March 2020

Contents

★

The Effect of Hearing the Sublime

Odysseus, who heard the sirens sing,
was not enraptured by another thing
he heard from human lips; fools muttering
and golden sounds that proved the flutist's skill,
which other men said gave their hearts a thrill,
to him were equally dislikable.
He knew that he would never hear again
the sounds he would have died for had his men
been able to hear what he said to them,
which was, "Steer toward the music, though it means
we shall not land upon familiar scenes
nor want to, once this music intervenes."

The Powow River Poets Anthology II

Meredith Bergmann

The Bird in the Bathroom

to my son Daniel

All gray, our bird was small but not a sparrow.
He huddled underneath the pipes. He'd been
alone for days, since those who'd let him in
had fled the flooded house, but locked each window.

Crouched there, uncoaxable as chronic sorrow,
our bird was silent and his eye looked dim.
I dropped a worn-out dishcloth over him
and shook the bundle out onto the meadow.

He hopped away, and someday you must follow,
from little rooms of therapy begin
to ask yourself what none of us can ask you.
One always dreams of more dramatic rescue,
like ours from flood: you soar through lashing wind.
The chopper sets you gently on your shadow.

Meredith Bergmann

That Fruit

First Eve, intended for eternal play,
played at a kind of gardening. Her soil
was hidden under tangled, tendriled vines
which she unpicked and rewove to array
the trees, and wound and spun each tight green coil
around her wrists, around their branching veins.
Sometimes, among those trees, she disappeared.
She'd wake from forty minutes' fragrant spell,
nails blackened, forearms stung, with something cleared
that talking to him would not heal. She loved
pretending that it mattered if a weed
grew tall. Those bouts of guilty pleasure left
her hankering for hard work, vital need.
She would taste anything to make that real.

Meredith Bergmann

From the New House

Our ground is frozen now, but when it thaws,
I will exhume my pet. It's my pet, now.
I want to know what someone thought to bury
so shallowly its vertebrae appear
one at a time, in puddles in the rain.

I want to know what joys ran through its brain,
and what it learned, perhaps too late, to fear,
and what it did to make itself look scary
and whether there are more around, and how
they run, and whether they have hooves or claws.

But do I want to own a living thing?
I used to cry into the velvet ears
of pointers, powdered against ticks, blood-warm,
and wrap my arms around their sleek, flecked hides.
We didn't bury them. We lived in town.

We took them to the vet to be put down.
Were they incinerated? Time divides.
To reassemble one, to grasp the form
of pet or predator, may take me years.
I need to think. I'll let it lie, till spring.

Meredith Bergmann

Period Furniture: The Royal Bedchamber

from "The Museum of Sex"

Nobody thinks that this is really Art.
It's just the stuff that dreams are made on, hung
with rich, explicit tapestries that chart
a dozen metamorphoses. Among
these flagrant scenes, intended to impart
a history for acts that all our young
discover, none alludes to what the heart
acquires. The role of marriage is unsung.

But beds are made. This took us many years.
The heyday in the blood seems nearly tame,
yet every spring supports and reaffirms
our passion's heft. The craft, the art that clears
a brow, ignites a laugh, can still inflame
this antique bed of wood made frail by worms.

Meredith Bergmann

Lost Wax

(after Edward Taylor's "Huswifery")

Make me a portrait of a self more fine
To cast me from myself to final form.
Rain down and moisten all the dust that's mine
And make me clay that you may knead and warm.
Then pack me round an armature of bone
Until you find the shape that is my own.

Then make the mold to copy me in wax.
I am my shape—my clay you may forget,
No matter if it dries and falls and cracks.
My just impression will survive me yet.
Then burn me out, so, deep inside your oven,
My wax is lost to let my void be proven.

This fireproof mold, of loving memory made,
May drink the boiling alloy of your grace
Of which I then consist. Your heat then fade
And let me harden. Break me out and chase
Away my imperfections. Make me well
That I, now hollow, ring. Make me your bell.

Wendy Cannella

The Word *Slut*

Look it up in the dictionary. It's newish,
right? Invented in the early 1980s
for those girls in the black-lace Madonna
gloves and torpedo bras. Wrong. *The foulest*
slutte of all ye towne strutted her stuff
in 1402. 1402, people. And I have more news
for you. *Slut* never meant *slut* until I used it
on myself. And I did. I tried it on for size
the year I lived alone in a smoky apartment
and since it really means *slovenly* I found it
heavenly, just right for the kind of messes
I craved constantly.
But what kind of asshole writes in his *Odes*:
       She's ugly, she's old . . .
       And a slut, and a scold.
That's Shenstone circa 1765 and thank God
he's no longer alive. Thank God for sluts like us
who want to feel our way down the body
of a word, want to bend it backward:
see how it can put out a candle, a guttering
slut; how it can leave little hard buttons of dough,
slut's pennies, in a loaf of bread, then gather
up its skirts, never worry about sweeping
a floor, puffs of *slut's wool* blowing everywhere
around us, the glorious dust our bodies
slough off—*sluttiness*, unctuous golden word,
a condition of living. J. Rice understood, when he

proclaimed in 1881, *My lord shall marry
this extravagant slut!* Were we all to bring our
lordhood into the lower extravagances.

And had there been a word for my mother's lover
with as much power as the earth-shattering *slut*
that cracked my parents' house down
the middle. And what if we could go back
to the 1600s when *slut* became a term
of endearment for children, you dearest
darling, *thou art a sweet slut,*
Landor wrote in *Imaginary Conversations.*

I'm not making this up. Once you know
a word, you can't unknow it, even if
you take it back, and you try to love it.

Wendy Cannella

Message from a Dead Pearl Diver

Benjamin Paul Akers, *The Dead Pearl Diver* (1858)

Don't get so close   quit staring   haven't you
ever   seen a dead man go stone   haven't you   studied
the neoclassical period   I'm just like every other   frozen
numbskull   baring my torso   arching my back   penny-
smooth   can't you   read? the sign says   DO NOT
TOUCH   anyway I can't give you   what you want
you're starting   to remind me   of something   your
little blue   purse snapped   shut   under   your   arm   I'm
so tired   of my own   dramatic   gestures don't you see
the museum guard   over there   please step back   from
the mesh net of my despair   leave my messages unopened
oysters   I   dug   out   of   the muck don't   tell   me   I
did it   for money   I   was   flooded   by   the body's
many   doors   I ended each day   with a mouthful of
~~sand~~   pearls   ~~sand~~

Michael Cantor

Tree Swallows in August

At first it all seems random, then each day
another group appears, till by degrees
their black-and-whiteness fills the Refuge skies
and scattered banks and swoops of anarchy
give way to groups that practice in-line, tree-
top passes—now swallows swarm and sweep in free
yet structured flight, now soar in symmetry:
two separate flocks merge upward joyfully.

"Bank left," I shout, and tilt to show them how.
"Pull yourselves together—nose to tail—
THERE IS NO 'I' IN 'SWARM.'"
                                        Their V takes sail,
and on the Refuge road, I take a bow
to plaudits from the passing cars, then hear,
"That imbecile is back again this year."

Michael Cantor

The Love of Sushi Sue

I lived near Tokyo's Hama-Zushi bar,
those years I was a seafood sybarite—
would start off there with monkfish caviar
and sweet live shrimp, to set the appetite,
then grab a cab to narrow streets where night
rolled into dawn, and hunt for something more.
I'd often wander home about first light
to find Old Hama, sweeping out his store.
He'd eye my catch that wiggled past his door,
but knew my true love was an artful blow-
fish broth, or chunks of fatty tuna, raw,
caressed with strands of gleaming herring roe.
Good food was all I worshipped and revered
and women, though amusing, interfered.

In time, the real-life girlfriends disappeared,
replaced by fantasies of Sushi Sue
who, naked as a salmon, commandeered
my reveries—slim sushi ingenue
enshrined behind Old Hama's bleached bamboo.
She worked like nude quicksilver, with a blade
in each small hand: Hama's fish swam through
her fingers and in seconds were filleted,
embraced by rice and seaweed, and arrayed
with fat carp's heads and pouting silver bream—
sea urchin eggs, fresh squid and trout—displayed
as backdrop for my slick, wet ocean dream.
But Sue repelled me when I cupped her breast:
"A sushi girl cannot make love to guest!"

Although all that was years ago, the quest
remains. My thoughts have never wandered far
from Hama's pickled prawns with lemon zest,
the earthy taste of slow-baked arctic char—
or Sushi Sue's small room behind the bar—
where I now nibble her *hirame*, coax
the sweetness from her *uni*, feel a star
ignite within me as she lightly strokes
my *ana-kyu*, and whispers private jokes.
The night moves on from sake sips to nips
and licks of salty flesh whose taste evokes
a sigh—and *mirugai*—from parted lips.
"I'm glad that you like raw fish," she will coo,
as I finally taste the love of Sushi Sue.

Hirame: Halibut. Often served as a sashimi-style first course, with a
ponzu dipping sauce (lime juice, soy sauce, and sake).

Ana-kyu: A conical, handmade sushi specialty of rice, cucumber strips,
and grilled ocean eel, topped with a thick, sweet sauce and rolled
in seaweed. They are almost impossible to eat without dripping the
impenetrable sauce on your wrist, and devotees wear these stains
as badges of honor, like the nicotine-drenched fingers of post-war
French intellectuals.

Uni: Sea urchin gonads.

Mirugai: A large clam, analogous to a New England quahog.

Michael Cantor

To an Old Friend Who Died Young

The first time was a game, we all agreed,
a cry for help, of course, but nothing more
and then you dove out over Eighty-Seventh Street.

The maid was due at noon—you gambled she'd
smell gas as soon as she came near the door—
that first time was a game. We all agreed

you missed your ex; you shrugged, you blamed the weed
and promised us there would be no encore—
but then you broke apart on Eighty-Seventh Street

that Sunday morning. What voices did you heed,
what madness crept up to the fourteenth floor?
The first time was a game, we all agreed;

we spoke of how you always seemed to need
attention; called up stunts you'd staged before—
and then you sailed out over Eighty-Seventh Street,

and gave the game an ending guaranteed
to make it clear who kept the final score.
The first time was a game, we all agreed;
and then you plummeted to Eighty-Seventh Street.

Lament

A day or two ago I tried to quote
Camus on modern man: "He defecates
and reads the Sunday papers," I first wrote—
but what it should have been was "fornicates,"
and "Sunday" was my fantasy. So this
is what it all comes down to—thoughts of shits
and weekends with the *Times* invade a kiss-
kiss-fuck-fuck bang-bang mind as age submits
his calling card, engraved, upon a bone-
white plate: a view ahead of weekly crossword
strugglings, and bits and scenes from well-known
films, and scraps of other voices, overheard
as life retold. *He grows old.* I grow old,
and treasure all these things, and fear the cold.

Michael Cantor

For Harry, Who Had Three Passports

I knew a man, who had a man, who knew
a man inside the Ministry. He said
his man was just the man to see you through

whatever difficulties might ensue
in sorting out the living from the dead.
I knew a man who knew a man. Who knew,

back then, what Harry really knew, or who
he'd ever helped, or who got screwed instead?
He was the kind of man who'd see you through

his pale blue eyes, and sense at once what you
most feared—and what you'd pay to ease your dread—
to meet a man who knew the man who knew.

I'm just a businessman, he'd say, *a Jew
without a tribe*—and raise his gleaming head—
but you can trust my man to see you through.

When others raged, he quietly withdrew,
and we all left, but Harry never fled:
he knew a man, who knew a man, who knew
the man who was the man to see you through.

My Fault Lines

Clumsy bumbled in, inept.
Heedless tumbled when she leapt.
Presumptive trod and overstepped.
Lazy's late. She overslept.

Ditherer will make you wait.
Pessimist is blaming fate.
Carper's sharpened words berate.
Nervous? In another state.

Smarty-pants holds up her hand.
Loudmouth always beats the band.
Bossy barks a rough command.
Prideful thinks she's simply grand.

Ditzy's world is all her own.
Absent-minded lost her phone.
Nosy's snout is overblown.
Lusty needs a chaperone.

Interrupter's barging in.
Procrastinator won't begin.
Martyr takes it on the chin.
Blameless hides behind her grin.

Barbara Lydecker Crane

Conjuring a Son

Mom asks, "How's your son?"
each time I visit now, though
I've never had one.

She asks it loudly,
sweetly crinkling eyes as if
she knows I'll proudly

tell his latest news:
Timmy learned to stand today—
Tim can tie his shoes

(or should he be Hugh?).
He'll have dinner with you, Mom,
soon as soccer's through—

a bike, a moped—
he grew before we knew it.
He's thinking premed

(now I see him: Nick . . .
he's tall, shy, wry, and enrapt
with geriatrics).

He's up for a Nobel!
Mom, every day Nick's at work,
he's wishing you well.

Barbara Lydecker Crane

Shards of Knowing

Czech Republic, May 2017

She gives us only shards of what she knows
about this former forced labor camp.
"I live nearby. I volunteer, and this
is just my second week as guide," says Marta,
as she strokes her tiny necklace cross.

She gives our tourist group an overview
of how and when the Soviet regime
imprisoned Czechs suspected of dissent.
"For cooks and guards, they hired locals. But,"
she's quick to add, "Soviets ran the camp.

"They forced the men to mine uranium
for bombs, and hundreds died from radiation."
Marta shows us rusted trams on tracks
that carted out the blackened mining waste
into a looming mound beyond the fence.

Pointed posts and corner sentry towers
punctuate the lines of thick barbed wire.
Someone asks if prisoners escaped.
"One did," the guide replies, "but seven more
were shot and killed, here or at the border."

There's silence. I ask her softly if she had
a relative imprisoned here. She pauses,
then reveals, "I had a grandfather here
for years. I don't know much about his time."
She straightens up: "Please follow me inside."

The little library's packed with party tracts.
I picture a gaunt old man who's more than willing
to sit and read anything at all.
While our guide decries indoctrination,
Stalin, from his frame, listens in.

Down some steps and ducking heads to enter,
we cluster then in claustrophobic dark
to hear, "The Hole, the harshest punishment.
Imagine summer heat," Marta murmurs,
"or sleeping on this bare concrete in winter."

We shiver under a steel gray sky while trooping
to a barrack. "Sometimes, to break their minds,"
our guide relates, "the guards forced men to stand
beside their bunks all night. If someone dozed,
the guards bellowed and banged against the bars."

I almost glimpse a gray-haired sleeper sway
as we're taken to the hospital, a room
with beds, cabinet, table, one white coat.
"A prisoner was admitted," Marta winces,
"only if he'd lost the strength to walk."

Our guide is looking spent herself. Tour done,
I thank her and she leans her head to mine:
"My Deda . . . a barrack guard eleven years . . .
to feed his children." Marta's voice breaks.
She turns away, head down and shoulders hunched.

Rain begins to pelt the gravel walk
and I scurry to the bus, the last to board.
The guide gives a wave akin to a salute.
We pull away as Marta stands stock-still
and shrinks inside the camp's open gate.

Robert W. Crawford

The Empty Chair

Out on the rocky point there stands a white
And isolated Adirondack chair.
The tourists take a snapshot of the sight—
But only if nobody's sitting there.

I guess they know, without fine arts degrees,
The standard first-term lesson, "less is more."
It's all about the possibilities
And the importance of the metaphor.

The focus isn't on the lovely ring
Of blue in which the empty chair is framed—
Where ocean meets the sky—it's on the thing
That in an artful picture can't be named:

They save a central place for what might be—
A certain absence, looking out to sea.

Robert W. Crawford

Kitchen Remodeling

I know I should be listening to your
description of the changes that you've made,
since you implied that following this tour
I'd take the test to be your kitchen aide.
I should note where you've moved the lobster pot,
but I'm distracted by your lips, your smile,
the way your hips rest up against—well, not
your hips exactly—the edge of cool white tile.
I know you're telling me about the brand
new island and the cabinet space inside,
but it's a blur. I hope you'll understand,
forgive the fact that I've grown glassy-eyed,
and lost, imagining what I could do
on this expanse of countertop with you.

Robert W. Crawford

What Matters Here

An atom's 99.9%
nothing at all. The world's an empty place.
Its solid shapes are objects we invent
to give a form to nuclei and space.
But these constructions aren't exactly fake—
it hurts when, as a test, we kick a stone;
electrons charge across the void and make
illusions hard enough to break a bone.
Outside the window, photons waver, glow,
collapsing to what matters here: your bright
blue scarf, dark hair; a body that I know
is not a trick of late November light.
You and I—more than a thought, thin air—
unique arrangements of what isn't there.

Robert W. Crawford

A Passenger

SF Hydro, 20 February 1944

You do not know what lies within the hold.
Calmly, you walk the deck while down below
clocks tick toward their appointed hour. You go
about your business, unaware of bold
decisions, grand designs; obey when told
to show your papers. Soon, plastique will blow
apart the ferry's bow. You'll never know.
You simply note the night has gotten cold.

But if you knew what this trip held in store,
would you still see the beauty of the moon?
The rising haloed moon that just now broaches
a mountain pass above the darkened shore
and, full, resplendent, sends a white harpoon
across the water as your hour approaches.

Grappling Hook

That summer I was eight, or nine, up early
to help my grandpa coming back at dawn.
I saw it on the transom of the boat—
an anchor-sized, steel-gray, and three-pronged hook
still wet and covered with the lake debris.
"What's that?"
           He hesitated, trying to decide
if I was old enough to handle it.
"It's called a grappling hook. You drag it on
the bottom of a lake to find a body.
We needed it to find a boy that drowned."

I saw exactly as it happened, like a movie
where they had a light that wasn't there
in the real world. The boy, his eyes closed, full
of water, out of air, rocking in the silt.
The grappling hook came out of the inky brown
and with a lurch hit him and his eyes opened.
"Did he reach out and grab the line?" I'd seen
a woman at the shore lunge for a float
a lifeguard tossed to save her from the waves.

"No. He was dead already." He looked at me,
his face a mix of anger and confusion,
"Some Brown's Mills teenagers were camping out,
and then the stupid, silly boy went swimming,
right after dinner, toward the middle island—
and halfway out I guess he got a cramp.
To think!—just to show off to a girl."

Robert W. Crawford

Hawks in the Leaves

The silly chickens huddle in dismay.
Each shadow cast by falling leaves they take
to be a hawk descending on its prey.
They're scared, while I'm just resting on my rake.
Today's the stripping day, when in a blink
our postcard fall receives its fatal blow.
Some blame the southwest wind. I'd like to think
the leaves themselves know when to go.

And so the hens and I believe there's more
to this world than meets the casual eye. A whiff
of woodsmoke and the closing of a door:
I don't know all that's happening here—as if
a child's still hiding in that pile of leaves,
or something's perched up there, along the eaves.

Sonnet with Horse

A quatrain made of one strong rhyme and glue
to hold the lines that long to fly apart;
a weaker rhyme that somehow has to do;
a horse that hates to pull its racing cart.

Another quatrain stronger than the first,
appealing to the senses—something red
flutters from its mane while bubbles burst
inside the spittle hanging from its head.

A volta taking us from there to here
while the horse rebelliously plods;
one good turn deserves another near
a final couplet written by the gods:

these enterprises fit our grand design
if horse and sonnet reach the finish line.

David Davis

Larkspur

All the cows were facing north but one.
Larkspur was her compass. As she ate,
the drug compelled her to stare at the sun,
to kick and howl and fiercely ruminate.
She spent the night hallucinating hay
and milky ways and blazing waves of grain.
She saw the young males deftly led away
and felt the current coursing through each brain.
Why should the cows depend on metal hands
to steal the fluid before their udders ache?
Why should the fences limit where each stands,
and why does this seem normal when awake?
Larkspur drew these uncowlike thoughts forth
but when it faded she knew to face north.

David Davis

The Waterfall

I left my cubicle and those gray things—
the bugs we couldn't fix, the deadlines passed—
to drive four hours and camp near Poncha Springs,
well off a road I always took too fast.

Next day I ate and left at dawn to hike
a trail I chose at random from a map.
Passed once too often by a mountain bike,
I left the path and climbed the ridge. A gap

opened on a way down to a stream.
I followed it, and then I heard a sound.
Aspen-dappled, moving in a dream,
I ducked beneath limbs, made my way around

the powdered trunks and fairy trumpet stalks,
the cinquefoil and columbine and rose,
toward a booming coming from the rocks.
A final wall of briars tore my clothes.

I broke through to a pool beneath a falls,
a hidden place that no one ever knew.
Reverberating thunder filled the walls
of rock that hid the waterfall from view.

I do not know how long I stood in mist
and sound and memory with my mind caught
on something that, somehow, my life had missed
with no awareness of the loss—the thought

that earthbound streams can leap into the air,
turn into rainbows falling like bouquets,
in roaring coruscated land, prepare
for normal life, grow calm, and flow away.

David Davis

The Juggler

I juggle what life gives me in an arc
that rises overhead: news from the media,
a subprime mortgage, marriage, a bad spark
plug, a three-foot long encyclopedia.
I bite the apple as it flashes by,
lick a stamp and stick it to a letter,
poke thread into a silver needle's eye,
tune the engine so it idles better.
Then I myself am tossed up to the skies
to join the objects that I have just thrown.
I struggle to control them as I rise,
to make their orbits orbit me alone,
for I am juggled as I juggled them
and, juggled, must start juggling again.

Dawn

The early morning flaring of the skies
roars overhead as dawn grows out of black.
Through the dilated pupils of my eyes
the colors strike my nerves and, farther back,
inside my grayish, convoluted brain,
the neurons fire, the sweet endorphins flow.
I wonder what advantages we gain
in being so affected by this show.
Science can't explain the way dawn feels.
It's not the goal of natural selection.
No other species sees these reds and kneels
and looks inside itself for like perfection.
To other animals it's simply light.
Dawn's a human word and human sight.

What Joseph Might Have Said

So, never mind that, *What would Jesus do?*
He preached, he healed, he saved—we've got him pegged.
It's Joseph who's the mystery man. It's true!
He never contemplated, spoke, or begged.
See, he was blessed in dreams with *angel-speak*.
When Mary came home pregnant, they told Joe
it was the work of God. And being meek,
ole Joseph took her in and watched her grow.
When angels told him, *Flee*, he packed his kin,
whisked them away until the coast was clear.
And when the hit man Herod was all in,
the angels said, *Go home*. Joe didn't fear.
But what was it that Joseph could've thought?
Oy gevalt! Such a life I've got!

M. Frost Delaney

When You're Left Behind

It's like his truck seen in the distance, dim.
You focus on the road ahead. It's dirt
and desolate with empty plumes of dust.
Reality sets in—you'll be an ex—
as sun reflects off fading bumper chrome:
the life that really was, and what was not.

It happens way too fast. His tires spin,
the motor torques, and in an instant years
together drop into your well of tears,
confirmed when final overdrive kicks in.

And, yes. . . . The atmosphere was getting hot,
but not with pillow talk. There was no "home"—
just battles over money, moving, sex.
You do not see the marriage going bust,
the gaps of silence, scorching with such hurt
to blister love away from you, from him.

Horizon looms there up ahead; a drone
of fading motor leaves you all alone.

M. Frost Delaney

Silence

> . . . a spoon, a glove, a clock at its dull task,
> seem ominously edged, as if they knew
> secrets they might tell, if you could ask. . . .
> —Rhina P. Espaillat, "Observation"

What secrets hide in dishes in the hutch?
Or in the window coverings, the shades
pulled down? And what about those hardwood floors?
If they could whisper tales, would they tell much?

The stories they could weave into the braids
of time: the anguish cloaked behind closed doors,
the light that's blocked so no one really sees,
the tiptoes felt so someone can't be heard.

There had been two unhappy—no, scared—wives
abandoning all praying on their knees,
then passing on before there came a third.

She took to hiding keys and all the knives,
and never wore her shoes when in the house.
The nights he raged—threw cups and bowls and plates—
she cowered in a corner, held back tears,
and wondered why she stayed with such a spouse,
and worried if she'd meet the past wives' fates.

Like them she was a prisoner of her fears.
But dishes, shades, and floors will never tell.
They know intimidation all too well.

Rhina P. Espaillat

After

Of all my images of you, is this—
or that—the one to keep? The sick old man
I washed and fed and diapered like a child,
and eased to sleep with morphine and a kiss;
young, playful father; master artisan;
teacher; author of letters to the press
in which your conscience spoke, unreconciled
to the denial of justice; mandolin-
strummer who chose me for a wife;
soldier home from the front, aged, though still less
than twenty-one, and aching to begin—
given this second chance at life—your life.
You gave yourself to me, with ring and vow.
I kept all of you then. I mean to now.

Rhina P. Espaillat

Just Stopping

The god in whom I once believed
showed up last night beside my bed,
and sat down at the foot. I said,
"What a surprise! Lord, I'm relieved
that you're not dead!"

He shrugged. "I have good days and bad.
When I was Zeus, what clout I had!
These days, it's all about complaints.
What thanks we get—it makes me mad—
goes to the saints

for curing stuff and granting things,
as if Creation were a mall
where every merchant has his stall.
And arguments: *you're made of strings,*
you're a big ball

of motion, you're a state of mind,
you're mathematics . . . on and on."
Now I could see his face was lined
like that of some old Mafia don
whose turf is gone.

And he looked tired, which, truth to tell,
he'd have to be by now, and bored,
unlike his counterpart in Hell,
and only fitfully adored.
He wasn't well.

I told him, "Look, you need some sleep;
lie down; I'll wake you when it's day,
and make you breakfast, if you stay."
But mumbling "... promises to keep ...,"
he paled away.

When light returned, I knew I'd done
less than I should. But then, he'd run
too soon to hear what or how much
I might have said: *Thanks for the sun*,
or *Stay in touch*.

Rhina P. Espaillat

On the Promenade

A memory: one brisk fall day,
my mother, elegant in gray,
though very old, straight as a rod,
went walking on the Promenade.

Widowed, confused, dimly aware
of who I was beside her there,
but fond of mischief, and still pretty.
She loved the river and the city,

seagulls and sailboats skimming by.
That afternoon she caught the eye
of an old fellow, bald and thin,
who gripped his cane and slipped right in

between us, like a trusted friend.
We strolled the boardwalk end to end,
we three, at ease, each way and back,
by the sun-speckled Merrimack.

No word was said, no look exchanged.
But as if they had prearranged
to rendezvous right there, right then,
the next day we were three again.

How lovely, after all these years,
this flirting between two old dears,
I thought, and smiled, turning to see
how flushed and flattered she must be.

"Mama," I said, "you have a beau!
And speechless, you've impressed him so!"
"Nonsense," she snapped, serene and cold.
"He's boring, slow, and much too old."

Bra

What a good fit! But the label says Honduras.
Alas, I am Union forever, yes, both breasts
and the heart between them committed to US labor.

But such a splendid fit! And the label tells me
the woman who made it, bronze as the breasts now in it,
speaks the language I dream in; I count in Spanish

the pesos she made stitching this breast-divider:
will they go for her son's tuition, her daughter's wedding?
The thought is a lovely fit, but oh, the label!

And oh, those pesos that may be pennies, and hard-earned.
Was it son or daughter who made this, unschooled, unwedded?
How old? Fourteen? Ten? That fear is a tight fit.

If only the heart could be worn like the breast, divided,
nosing in two directions for news of the wide world,
sniffing here and there for justice, for mercy.

How burdened every choice is with politics, guilt,
expensive with duty, heavy as breasts in need of
this perfect fit whose label says Honduras.

Rhina P. Espaillat

Guidelines

Here's what you need to do, since time began:
find something—diamond-rare or carbon-cheap,
it's all the same—and love it all you can.

It should be something close—a field, a man,
a line of verse, a mouth, a child asleep—
that feels like the world's heart since time began.

Don't measure much or lay things out or scan;
don't save yourself for later, you won't keep;
spend yourself now on loving all you can.

It's going to hurt. That was the risk you ran
with your first breath; you knew the price was steep,
that loss is what there is, since time began

subtracting from your balance. That's the plan,
too late to quibble now, you're in too deep.
Just love what you still have, while you still can.

Don't count on schemes, it's far too short a span
from the first sowing till they come to reap.
One way alone to count, since time began:
love something, love it hard, now, while you can.

Midge Goldberg

Walking on Ice

Foot traffic on the lake's increasing lately.
The fishermen are out without a boat,
Building fires and drilling holes sedately
In the only thing that's keeping them afloat.

Some folks are skating, measurers who know
The thickness of the thing, the hard and soft
Of it. They don't mistake the ice and snow
For something magic keeping them aloft.

The only ones unsure out here are geese,
Who clamor cautiously onto the lake.
The fact that they can fly gives them no peace—
Their wing-and-prayer approach to what might break

Recalls what lies beneath, how footing changes,
How pressure builds and cracks and rearranges.

Midge Goldberg

Snowman's Code

Carrots are cool. So's coal.

Feet aren't everything.
  Just look at all those squirrels,
  mobile, yet squirrelly.

A sunny day
  is a mixed blessing.

Snow: it's what matters here.
  it's what you're made of,
  if someone makes you.

Angels are beautiful,
  but two-dimensional,
  created by taking away.

Be proud of lumpy hereness,
  made by hands that carry
  you, scoopful by scoopful,
  to this place, at this moment,
  patting you into existence.

At the U-Pick

Children call, insistent bird-like cries:
"Look, look," they say, and then, "Look, look," again.
The parents call back, deeper, slow replies.
We nod, having been where they have been.

An older couple, further down the row,
murmuring in voices growing frail:
the sound of things we know we'll need to know.
And all the while, berries fill the pail.

Breakfast Shift at the Inn

Cassie, her ponytail streaked blonde and black,
worked breakfast shift most mornings, five to ten—
the inn the one good place in town for tips.
So that meant she had weekend nights to drink
at the inn's pub, flirting with Tom, who owned
the corner stool when not out giving sleigh rides.
He was her best friend Tina's older cousin—
mellow or dumb, depending on the light.
They played a drinking game called Nail the Guests:
guess the state they're from or take a drink.
Tina, working the bar, would play along.
Cassie would win: an accent, brand of purse,
even the dye jobs helped. She'd miss sometimes,
just to take a shot and go outside
to find the constellations that she knew,
rising above the mountains to the south.

Later, they'd pile in Tom's truck, head through
the notch to Lincoln and the ski resorts,
or further south to bars at Plymouth State.
Cassie knew some people from her classes
but didn't bother trying to say hi:
"That's right, you're in my chem lab," blah, blah, blah.
She'd stick with Tom and Tina for a while,
then find a vacant corner, sip her beer,
and wait. When it was finally time to go,
she'd steer them out the door into the cold.
They'd laugh, watching their breath make puffs of heat
they'd walk through, just to have it warm their faces.
She'd drive them home, feel the darkened mountains
gather her up toward day and the breakfast shift.

Paper Town

> Agloe is a fictional hamlet in Colchester, Delaware County,
> New York . . . put onto the map in order to catch plagiarism . . .
> Agloe was known as a "paper town" because of this.
> —*Wikipedia*

People driving through look at the map,
the empty road, the map. They clean their glasses.
Not knowing anything about this trap,
nearby townsfolk shrug, when asked. Time passes.

Myths arise about the mill that closed,
families that were forced to move away.
All sorts of dire causes are supposed.
Day trips are planned, with cheese and cabernet,

to find anything left behind, to scout
for cellar holes, chimneys, a single door.
Since it's a shame to let a town die out
like that, someone decides to build a store,

painted in weathered tones of creams and grays,
hoping to recall the halcyon days.

Midge Goldberg

Telling

Each time it was retold, the story grew.
I tried to find the truth, to no avail.
What really happened no one ever knew.

My mother's version never gave a clue
of a first husband, no mention of betrayal
each time it was retold. The story grew,

however, when she died. He'd been untrue,
and drank, her friend said—made the marriage fail—
and that's what really happened. No one knew

she'd kept some photos that she'd cut in two:
the hand gently holding her waist was male,
telling a different story. So I grew

curious, and called him. "She'd have me do
her braid each night." So this—this one detail—
happened, at least to him. I finally knew

I couldn't know. The different points of view—
you can't remove the teller from the tale.
Each time it was retold, the story grew.
What really happened no one ever knew.

Hades Creek, Washington

There was a time he only wrote for her.
She was the reason for his songs,
   and they were happy for a while.

Then she encouraged him to share his art
and he began to sing their love at shows.
   She felt a little selfish pride

that she could have what others wanted so.
But soon he spent such time away from her
   and she began to feel alone.

The house, his songs, their wealth were not enough.
She loved the man—of that she had no doubt—
   and they had been happy once, she thought,

before her aunt had said, "You cannot trust
an artist to stay faithful to his wife."
   Her words rang true, like prophecy.

Soon jealousies would crowd out all her love,
a nest of vipers living near her heart.
   And soon she gave in to despair.

She moved her things into the basement rooms
while he was out on tour with brand new songs
   he called *The Weeping of the Trees*.

The house felt like a tomb when he came back
and he did not expect to find a dog,
   with eyes like flashing fire, there.

Each night he sent her messages, and prayed
his songs were strong enough to see him through
    the restless days and sleepless nights.

In time, he put the guardian dog at ease
and made his way into this other world
    (or so it felt to him that night).

He waited there for her to notice him.
He was alone with her, no songs to help,
    only the echoes of his breath.

And she no longer seemed to be the woman
who once had echoed through the singer's songs,
    some woman in her place,

as if the woman he had known so long—
uncertain yet infinitely patient—
    had been replaced with someone else.

Then finally she spoke. She welcomed him
but like some guest. He sat with her. They laughed.
    She said she thought that she might try.

He offered her his hand. She wavered then.
"You go ahead," she said. "I'll follow you."
    With greedy steps, he made his way

and heard the echoing of his own steps.
Atop the stairs, he looked down for her
    and saw that she was gone for good.

Distances

My memory of you still rests upon
my shoulder, whispering sweet tales and lies
that sound so much like truths; I agonize
as day slowly becomes hard night, then dawn.

Then restlessly I find myself redrawn
in stark relief to see the lightened skies:
another day without you slowly dies.
But I cannot accept that you have gone.

Despite myself, I feed this little you,
longing for some peace to comfort me:
I hope you'll change your mind but know your heart

will not be satisfied, could not make do
with "us." There's so much world for you to see.
Your path through life is yours, alone, to chart.

Backup Plan

If I were single once again
(not that I'm really planning, dear),
I would indulge! Like other men,

I'd bag the low-fat regimen
and live on burgers, ribs and beer.
If I were single, once again

there would be Fritos in the den,
and napkin rings would disappear.
I would indulge like other men,

not shave or floss, and sleep past ten.
My feelings could be insincere.
If I were single once again,

and free to leave the seat up when
my heart desired, it is clear
I would indulge like other men—

although I would be helpless then,
and yearn for your return. I fear,
if I were single once again,
I would indulge like other men.

A.M. Juster

Proposed Clichés

Softer than an old potato
too moldy to mash.

More user-friendly than a hooker
hard up for cash.

Love is like a hard-time sentence—
but better than cancer.

Ask not what your country can do,
for fear of the answer.

Beauty beheld is merely skin-deep;
infections are deeper.

The price of honesty is steep;
candidates are cheaper.

A drowning man may clutch at straws,
but his sipping is pathetic.

Burn the candle at both ends
if you want to wax poetic.

You can call off your dogs,
but your cats will ignore you.

If actuaries had wings,
they still would just bore you.

An apple a day keeps the doctor away,
but not your disease.

Blood is thicker than water
except when they freeze.

It's all spilt milk under the bridge,
so don't be big babies.

If you're crazy like a fox,
get tested for rabies.

Love Song

from *Rapture with Paperclips* (2003)

They say you have to love yourself
to love another
and so for you, dear,
only for you,
I am focusing on myself.

I wore my silk pajamas all day long
in case the moment was right.
Mid-morning, yellow roses arrived;
I was touched by my gesture,
but before long
they wilted in the kitchen window.
Later, there was chocolate—
rich, *erotic* chocolate—
but within minutes it made me feel fat.

A passionate note to myself
only ignored my issues,
and I never seem to talk
to myself anymore.
I have become insensitive to my own needs.
Perhaps, my love, the answer
is couples therapy.

(after the English of Billy Collins)

Houseguests

There's shouting by the stove (it's Plath & Hughes)
as Wystan wanders off without his shoes
and Whitman picks the Cheetos off his beard.
The Ginsberg-Larkin chat is getting weird,
for after countless hours they have found
bizarre pornography is common ground.
Old Emily is not
as prim as billed—
when Dylan finds her bra-hooks—
she is thrilled.
Poe strokes his bird; Pound yawps that it's a pity
that T.S. can't sleep without his kitty.
Rimbaud's on eBay searching for a zebra
while sneering, "*Oui*, a *cheemp* can write *vers libre*!"
The Doctor's soggy chickens start to smell
and Wallace has insurance he must sell.
The readings are spectacular, I know,
but is there any way to make them go?

Fugitive Son

The Japanese mourn children they abort.
In Shinto shrines they pick a figurine
to represent the life that they cut short.
They bow, then slide a folded note between
the sandalwood and jade as if a soul
that never loved a face could now forgive
or any act of penance could control
unwanted visits from a fugitive.

I never picked a message I could send
or bargained for forgiveness. There was none.
Although I know my boy does not intend
more pain, he asks about the nameless son
we lost three months before he was conceived.
I have no words to tell him how we grieved.

Don Kimball

William, 1949–1966

On Sunday morning you will drown,
fate tossing us four instead of five:
the task, so early in our lives,
to dredge the depths of life foreshortened.
What author worth his name, unless
it only be his first attempt,
and he, some minor deity
still incomplete—like you and me—
could write you off in Chapter One?
Yes, you, who must have seemed the best,
the brightest, proud protagonist!
A bitter tale, in which you're dead:
the book I wish I'd never read.

Don Kimball

Journal of a Flatlander

Scribbled
on a three by five
while waiting for the others
to climb down from the tower on Oak Hill

I am convinced my fear of heights
is more genetic than one likes
to think. As much as others try,
I will not be talked out of it
as much as I would like. My people,
I'm certain, once their boots were tied,
not once lost their slow pace, nor left
the earth until the day they died.
My people, I'm convinced, not being
warriors, explorers, plowed precise
parallel lines behind great teams
of horses; apple-faced farmers, who,
instead of hiking high peaks, which
would dwarf or stymie them, stone-walled
the valleys in between; yet always
proud and sure of foot as mules.
People of some means, yes—though not,
I fear, your people of great heights.

Don Kimball

Birch

Now, burdened by the drag of heavy snow
grasping its gaunt old trunk, my birch must go.
Where once it stood amid an isle of flowers,
it stoops alone, unbraced against snow showers.
This statesman, in a compromised position,
cannot be propped or saved, has no ambition
except to bend the rules and block the way
while we the people plot an arbor day.
Old American Gray, you haven't a prayer;
the end of a long, unhappy love affair!
As I apply my chainsaw's jagged smile,
reducing you to slash, a punk wood pile—
birches beware: you're bound to lose your place
to Japanese Maple, or a parking space.

Burial for a Stray

for B. B.

Two dogs and a cat who knew you best
came by and sat as I dug a hole.
Azaleas bloom there where you rest.
Two dogs, a cat, who knew you best,
keep vigil here: at whose behest?
Torn ear, one eye: life takes its toll.
Two dogs and a cat who knew you best
came by and sat. I dug the hole.

Joan Alice Wood Kimball

On First Looking at Rembrandt's
The Shipbuilder and His Wife

(after John Keats)

Of couples, many portraits have I seen
that showed them holding stiff, their gaze
at me, so forced—with pitchfork, standing, lean,
or seated, plump, in satin robes and lace,
or leaving Eden, nude except for fig tree leaves,
or praying at a cradle in a stable.
There was a static quality. The sitters had to freeze
to let the painter work his chosen fable.
Consider my surprise to see, by chance,
a classic artist's quite eccentric portrait
of a man and wife in momentary stance:
he, startled; she, bursting with a rushed report. It
limned such fleeting action that they can't
have posed for long, not even for Rembrandt.

Joan Alice Wood Kimball

Hypatia, 415 CE

Where are ink and parchment?
I remember every moment:
the last time my feet braced a floor,
the tonsured holy man who grabbed Beta's bridle.

I dismissed my waiting students with a shout
and lost the reins as another brute
sprang into the chariot, ripping my scholar's cloak.
A third monk pulled me naked from the cart's edge.
The thief in the chariot tossed my bound notes
to Bishop Cyril's shouldering horde
who tore them for tinder.

Dragged before the Caesarian altar,
I was dismembered like a pagan marble.
They butchered my legs in conic sections,
scored my skin with broken tiles
while I garnished their habits in blossoming scarlet.
Before they threw my pieces on the Kinaron fire,
my heart's breath fled.

On the church flags, pooled with my sap,
they missed one ripped ear lobe
and here, under a subsellium, my severed thumb.
I trace the digit's stump: a bloodied ellipsis.
Unlike Isis, I cannot reassemble me.
I will never be interred as Theon
with myrrh and music.

Where are ink and reed?
I must affirm Synesius's notion of the Afterward.
His fellow Christians err in the details, though.
I will record it.

Oh, where   is   ink?

Joan Alice Wood Kimball

Chauvet Cave

She pulls charcoal
in wide sweeps,
shades cheekbone,
gives the eye unlidded glare,
the jaw a hint of hunger.

Her cave lion profile
flickers in firelight
as it watches three bison,
one above the other,
on a rough rock wall.

From memory's retina
she sketches the head
staring, alert,
draws a dotted muzzle,
mouth ajar.

She is Old Woman
with a single white hair
on her chin.
She is Child reaching
high on ten toes.

She is Lens that freezes motion,
Seed that conquers death,
Hand that startles a trekking heart
thirty-six thousand years hence.

Joan Alice Wood Kimball

Rhymes from a River

(after Christian Wiman)

A stream so blue it mimics the sky,
A dawn, a golden scar.
A chain of mallards drifting by,
A chain of geese afar.

A willow shading bloated spill
Above a quick mink's wake.
A tethered rowboat not quite still,
A glint of water snake.

A tree crown shading early light,
A red root sucking mud.
A sap vein coursing its full height
Above the river flood.

A human touch, the dock protrudes,
An angle thrusting out,
A wooden stage for solitude,
A span to nurture doubt.

Jean L. Kreiling

Winter Boats

Becalmed in backyards, cold and mortified,
boats hold their breath until the day when stiff
blue tarps can be removed, when bows can glide
across blue bays. For months, the sleekest skiff
looks clumsy, inconvenienced by her own
unfloated weight, bound to a rusty trailer,
as buoyant as an old shoe or a stone,
when she should be bound only to a sailor.
But he's a summer creature too: he knows
how briefly hulls and hearts are light, how short
the breathing season is. It's he who tows
her, come the fall, to this ignoble port
beside the shed; he leaves her high and dry
and heavy with a longing for July.

Jean L. Kreiling

No Escape

He guns the engine, just to hear it roar:
a barrel-chested, thunderous last word.
He'd slammed out of the house, but that screen door
had barely slapped. Now, sure that he's been heard,
he takes off, elbow out the window, aping
his father's driving posture, unaware
that so much of what he thinks he's escaping
has hitched a ride, has filled his tires with air,
has fueled the bellowing of his V-8,
and now glares in his windshield. Peering past
blind rage, he sees enough to navigate
around the potholes, and goes nowhere fast.
His left forearm, like that of his old man,
will always wear a slightly darker tan.

Jean L. Kreiling

Left Out

It starts that Wednesday when believers bear
their faith in forehead smudges, and my brow
is pagan-pale. And then they all compare
what they'll give up for forty days, and how
they'll binge on those things later. When they claim
to know that their redeemer lives, I sigh
with envy, even feel a twinge of shame,
because I just don't get it. If I lie—
partake of alleluias and baked ham
as if they mean what they're supposed to mean—
then they don't taste the way they should; the sham
leaves ashes on my tongue. I haven't seen
the light, I don't believe he did ascend
to heaven—but I wish I could pretend.

Jean L. Kreiling

Ovillejo for the Librarian

"Four weeks," she says, as she hands back
a stack
of books checked out to me   bound herds
of words
I'll milk all month. It's life she lends,
and friends
to share it with. Though she pretends
they're only pages, I can sense
she knows she gives me sustenance:
a stack of words and friends.

Jean L. Kreiling

Brahms on Interstate 95

"All the heart wants is to be called again."
—Rhina P. Espaillat, "Rachmaninoff on the Mass Pike"

I'm south of Boston when I hear the first
huge thuds of timpani, and I'm immersed
in waves of urgent sound. Although I stay
alert to passing semis, and don't stray
from my lane, Brahms's first symphony demands
attention. So again my heart expands
to heed this artful call, its every tone
as satisfying as a rhyme, well known
but not predictable, not quite. Because
tread wears and time relaxes nature's laws,
the same notes make a tune that's not the same,
despite its unchanged spelling—as my name
links constant letters to a self that varies
with every breath. Like me, the music carries
a shifting load, and after years of miles,
I don't imagine that it reconciles
the past and present, nor can Brahms remove
the billboards that I speed past, or improve
the strip-mall scenery. He only wrote—
in circumstances notably remote
from mine—some small black marks, a sort of code
interpreted by those who've breathed and bowed
his old ideas alive again, to sing
inside my car, my ear, my blood. They ring
in tune with all that hums in me already:

regrets as dark as cellos, faith as steady
as straight-stemmed quarter notes, riddles as dense
as dissonance. I'm not drawn by suspense—
I know exactly how this ends—but still
I have to listen, beckoned by his will
and my need. As I sit in my parked car,
well north of Boston now (I've traveled far
more distance than the map would show), I wait
to hear the final chords reiterate
C major: not exactly victory,
but resolution, made of harmony
that fills my lungs. My driving's more aggressive
these days, my search for cheap gas less obsessive,
but Brahms still calls my flesh and bones and cells,
and they reverberate like living bells.

Jean L. Kreiling

Children Playing on the Beach

(after Mary Cassatt)

Allowed to play beside the sea,
two small girls focus earnestly
on pail and shovel and their chore
of rearranging bits of shore.
The ocean's blue immensity

escapes their notice; they don't see
white sails that distantly agree
with each girl's tidy pinafore.
Allowed to play,

they shuffle the topography
with calm, sunburned intensity.
They don't converse, they don't explore,
they only sift the sand. The more
you watch, the more you long to be
allowed to play.

Nancy Bailey Miller

Suitcase

In my attic, several years ago,
a red squirrel gnawed worn fabric
on the navy suitcase that my mother
carried in her travels to Dubrovnik, Peking,
Moscow, Lake Louise.

A combination lock with tiny silver tumblers
spins to 8:15—it's curtain time on Broadway,
time to have a bite to eat at Sardi's.
But it's also time to pitch this suitcase
with the red-plush lining, still a hint

of scented soap—magnolia.
The elastic on the pockets now is stretched
and brittle; there is just one golden safety pin
attached to drooping silk.
In my mother's day, this lining cushioned

silk pajamas, silver flask of vodka,
purple ultra-suede that never wrinkled,
folded Catalina swimwear, and
a book or two, perhaps James Michener.
Could it be twenty years

since I sat near the gurney,
my last journey to the land of royal palms,
to kiss my mother's crayon-yellow forehead
just before she traveled to the fire
and the ashes?

Nancy Bailey Miller

Revisiting
"Something there is that doesn't love a wall"

But why can't we reroute the bird migration?
Insist on green cards from our waterfalls?
What monarch claims the path of butterflies
in spring? And honey bees? Why can't we stall
their journeys as we please—pollination
for the crops be damned! We'll soon return
all turtles without visas, strip-search vagrant
voles, and round up armored armadillos.
We'll detain coyotes holding stolen
cell phones, halt undocumented breezes.
We'll be great again, so safe and proud!
Until Creation splits a thundercloud.

Eden 1843

Abbie Alcott honored Bronson's schemes:
utopian farm, new home for their young brood,
until December came to freeze their dreams

of Eden. "Don't depend on cow nor teams
of horses for the plough, nor sheep for wool,"
said Bronson. Abbie honored all the schemes

while he went off to speak his vision. Means
for living from the land in summer could
beguile, until December froze those dreams.

Louisa May slept under attic beams
and played in orchards as her mother would
attempt to plant and honor Bronson's schemes.

Twenty shared the farmhouse, field, and streams,
but Abbie dug latrines, prepared the food,
until December came to freeze their dreams.

With the cupboard bare, the firewood gone, the reams
of books on tolerance—all in theory good,
mute on their shelves—she honored Bronson's schemes.
And still December came to freeze their dreams.

Anne Mulvey

Talking Back

At first, there was just one of you.
I couldn't have imagined two.
But then you said you had a son.
He was the only holy one.

By the time I'd reached the age of reason,
you'd convinced me it was treason
to doubt the holy trinity.
So then I had three gods I could not see.

I wish I hadn't been so slow.
I wish I had decided long ago
to listen to just one instead of three,
hearing less from you and more from me.

Anne Mulvey

Teen Angels: High Hopes, Circa 1960

We heard the bells that told us to wake up,
get dressed, eat breakfast. We followed bells
that told us where to go and when to kneel,
to pray, and even what to say. They chimed
in chapel time, Holy Mass, then school,
study hall, choir rehearsal, chores,
play till it was time to pray again,
dinner, dishes, silence, lights out, then sleep
till bells at dawn awake. Chime by chime,
those mundane bells kept track of earthly time.

Wedding bells had lured teen girls from home
to offer hearts and souls for perfect love.
Celestial bells had swept us off our feet.
Soon we'd be brides of Christ, and marry up.

Anne Mulvey

For Patricia, Whose Hair I Straightened in 1962

When you arrived, I wondered if you'd like
Ancilla Domini Convent School
where, like us, you'd wear blue serge
uniforms, so dark as to be black,
with white blouses. You'd live by bells,
have meals with all of us after grace,
do everything together.
Every six weeks, you'd be assigned
a new roommate. You'd have to keep your door
open all the time, both night and day.

Some doors cannot be easily opened.
Some currents cannot be stilled.
Even hair can be charged.
Your mother made the nuns promise
yours would be straightened every week.
I was chosen to care for your hair.

Saturdays at nine, I washed your hair,
rubbed pomade onto your waves
and reached in with a hot comb,
afraid I wouldn't get to the roots
or—worse—would singe the nape
of your neck, or scorch your scalp.
I know I burned you sometimes.
You'd cringe, but say, "It didn't hurt."
You never complained.

I wanted you to look the way
your mother would have liked.
I didn't want to pry.
One day, you were gone. Left.
I still wonder why.

Genealogy

The year that RFK and King were shot,
your father bought the last two hundred acres
from the youngest daughter of the German family
that tilled these hills for two fat centuries.
They'd built a barn, plain red (though when it rains,
the shadows of proud horses, names, and banners
push through the damp and show themselves), and added
a wooden summer kitchen to the house,
and earlier, the year of Gettysburg,
a set of rooms with foot-thick walls of rock.
Its core was laid by the Moravians
before the Revolutionary War:
they cleared the woods and tilled between the stumps,
put up a church—of which there is no trace,
not even a shallow, naked spot—and dug
a graveyard, now an unplowed bit of field.
The stones were carted off some years ago.
The Brethren whom they named remain in rows,
eroding as we speak, down to the ones
who died in combat with the Indians,
the Lenape, in the struggle for this land—
before those clans were flung beyond the ridges,
to Indiana, Kansas, and at last
to desiccated Oklahoma, dropping
the arrowheads that show like rocky shoots
at plowing, and the tonguing names of waters—
Saucony, Maxatawny, Tulpehocken.
A hundred people speak that language now.

What was this place before that time? The glaciers
palmed each valley, seam, and gully, leaving
the brittle tiers of greasy shale impressed
with the remains of vanished beasts and flowers.
Viewing them by the pond your father cut
is like perusing grimy photographs:
these are your ancestors, the trilobites—
your cousins, the bits of carapace and leaf
from when this farm took up the ocean floor.
But before that, where was this scrap of land?
The universe could have been no more than
a pebble, cinder, or a grain of clay:
the black dot in your uncreated eye.

The Frat Boys

Their shirtless bodies are frolicking again—
tackling each other in an April storm,
spendthrift with themselves, as only young men
can be. But it is not remotely warm.

The lawn is a snarl of pectoral and arm
in a game I cannot play, or even grasp.
However rough it seems, they mean no harm,
shoulder on shoulder in a perfect clasp

of biceps, deltoid, butt, and leather ball.
I want at once to gaze and be struck blind,
though it is not these boys I see at all.
At forty-four, and taken back, I find

myself once more with Adam S. and Marty A.—
strong-featured Adam, Marty blond as Thor—
in the prep school showers after class. They play
wet, naked soccer, and do not keep score.

Fuzz dirtying my belly and my thighs,
I was no ephebe, even at sixteen.
I lacked the ease of any of these guys,
then and now. And who could have foreseen

that Marty's chest, lamp-bright and just as clear,
along with each lithe feint and kick recalled,
would be squandered in a car crash in a year.
When last seen, Adam was aggrieved and bald.

It is not their bodies, but their carelessness
I marvel at—what these young men display.
I never will be able to possess
Adam and Marty capering in the spray.

James Najarian

The Annunciation

She expected nothing like it,
But pottered in her average day
Just like us; put some things away,
Scrubbed, tidied, lay about a bit,

Washed, glimpsed in a mirror—and then?
Then? Artists have yielded the scene,
Prodigaled drapery on a lean
Haloed angel, pristine—even

Stuck gigantic lilies in his hand,
Then painted Mary looking pale
And at the floor, the hail
Before Mary failing to land

Anywhere. Or they make
The angel a glint of light or wing.
Still, something is missing.
What was she feeling? An ache?

Fear? Fullness? A motion toward?
More than these. She took the braid
Of flesh and blade and spoke back, unafraid,
"I am the handmaid of the Lord."

Alfred Nicol

One Day

We walked in light and shade
along the lichened wall,
no task at hand
and nothing planned.
The poplar branches swayed.
And Finlay chased his ball.

And something made us smile,
and something else, again.
Nothing less
than happiness,
and good to last awhile.
Enough to last till when. . . .

This simple summer day
of not too much to do
may be the one
we look back on
when years have swirled away
and days like these are few.

Old Haunt

The book that taught *to dust shalt thou return*
collected dust, but I was quick to learn.
I thought that if I hastened my descent
I might avert some loss. So down I went

among the catacombs of libraries,
where Santayana questioned Socrates
in the hushed tone the newly dead assume
when they address their elders-in-the-tomb.

There I mixed in. Stiff and unathletic,
I fashioned a persona, The Ascetic,
that gained acceptance. All my gang were ghosts.
We raised an empty glass to make our toast.

Appearance didn't matter where we met.
Observing the unspoken etiquette
of disembodied voices, I kept still
and in the feast of silence had my fill.

It needed salt. But there was dust for that,
and at the empty table where we sat
plenty enough, for we were slight of build.
There were no table crumbs, and nothing spilled.

We would indulge a taste for subtleties,
and contemplate in long soliloquies
the ease of being none too full or fond
of anything or anyone. We'd bond,

these absences and I. Because I sensed
that what I felt they too experienced,
the opposite of a collector's greed,
something we shared of needing not to need.

Alfred Nicol

October 1962

"Up in the bathtub early . . ." Not at night.
"Get dressed, put on your brand new underwear . . ."
"Between your sisters on the couch, sit tight . . ."

"Come here a minute, let me comb your hair . . ."
This was an actual emergency,
although my baby brother didn't care

on mother's lap, where I wished I could be,
not looking at the television set.
Russia was gearing up for World War III

with JFK. Nobody'd shot him yet.
She spent the afternoon preparing us.
I guess we were prepared as we could get.

Maybe she pictured Mount Vesuvius?
Not an atom bomb, but still. The closest thing.
It would explain her making all the fuss.

She wouldn't quit, or waste time wondering
exactly what to do with one last day;
she planned for what the future still might bring

and tried to get us ready, in her way,
for when someone unburied our Pompei.

At Dusk

At dusk out on Plum Island, in October,
my friend and I sit on a ridge of sand
that overlooks the sea.
Indulging memory,
a child again, she takes her father's hand.
When she grows tired, he lifts her to his shoulder.

Slowly, now, a darkness fills the hollows.
Splotches of sunset founder in the rills.
Closing her eyes, she sees—
beyond the guava trees
along that inland, homeward path she follows—
La Vega in the shadow of its hills.

As for me, I grip the captain's wheel,
each salt air inhalation like a dram;
my dreams are all about
adventure, setting out—
until I feel myself adrift, off-keel,
and start the long way back to where I am.

We brace ourselves as we descend the dune,
caught up in time, itself a kind of tide,
whose whorls and eddies trace
the stories of a place.
Our footprints will get covered over, soon.
For now, they skirt the beachgrass, side by side.

Alfred Nicol

Nuts

I come in contact with a lot of nuts.
Poetry readings. Church. The library.
They're always there. Lost souls end up in ruts
like everybody else. I often see

a man whose armload of biographies
that codger won't live long enough to read,
fumbling for change to pay his past-due fees
on other Lives. How many does he need?

He's lost his place in his own story, one
thin volume more than he can carry home,
library-quiet, fording the Acheron.
And then there are the ruts that lead to Rome:

the crazies go to Mass on Sunday, too.
I've noticed torture going on. One fellow
brings the Inquisition to his pew.
His hair is matted, black. His eyes are yellow.

No "sign of peace." He won't let you come near.
His forehead's beaded from the fires he's fanning.
Bloodstorms. Paroxysms of guilt. I fear
his awful sin may be the one he's planning.

And poetry. Perhaps I shouldn't say.
The open mic's a magnet for the daft.
The trembling hand. The mangled, stiff cliché.
Time is a river; the podium's a raft

that poets grip, riding the floodwaters—let
the four winds blow! The struggling poets row
against the swells, bedraggled, cold and wet.
Forgive them, for they know not where they go.

Kyle Potvin

Diagnosis

Zero chance.
You know the truth; the blank walls taunt.
X-rays, sound waves, words dripping like drugs.
Will those sustain me?
Visitors offering cutlets, cashew butter, cider donuts.
Uttering a last Hail Mary, I think of my child
Terminally tied to me.
Statistical improbability—doctor shakes his head.
Radiation, I hear.
Queasiness, bloating.
Pump, forty-eight hours on a pump, I hear.
Options, there must be options!
No.
Me? Maybe surgery?
Let me believe, as I let my friend believe, there is hope.
Keep the faith, I told her
Just the other day.
I'll die.
How will I live?
Genes of damaged ancestors
Find me—
Ecstatic to survive, for awhile,
Dance around the room—
Catch me in the gut, the stomach.
Bigger than three tumors,
A silence.

Kyle Potvin

The Hard Work of Dying

The hospice nurse explained the letting go.
Give her space to do the work of dying.
On the sill, a green heirloom tomato,
brought in before the frost, sat there, sighing.
Or was that me, not knowing what to say?
Don't ask her things (such grief in giving up
exchanges!). *Back off engagement*—that way
we help her go. Tea grows cold in my cup.
Ten days since Emma took a sip of tea
or ate a slice of grape. She sleeps while rain
whispers a soothing chatter. The oak tree
clears its throat, weeping acorns in the drain.
Yellow snapdragons brighten up the room.
A day from now, they'll see a second bloom.

Kyle Potvin

To My Children Reading My Poetry after I'm Gone

If you are anything like me, you'll look
for clues about your mom inside this book.
You'll read each poem that I wrote and cry.
Please don't. You need to know it's such a lie.
That year when I was sick, I lost my hair.
I brought a cactus home: a prickly pear?
I think I only used that for the rhyme.
(That's why I made up stuff from time to time!)
That hulking boat that dreamed of more? It sank.
And graduation night—I *never* drank.
Some parts are real: I rocked you in my arms,
ate gyros, frites; my mother wore gold charms.
But poets play with words, ignore the truth,
"manipulate" as Plath once said. A ruth-
less cutting, blending, marking up—that's art.
Dears, best to trust what's written in your heart.

Fireball

At eight years old, I dodged the sisters' eyes:
ate my sandwich, then donned a saintly face,
walked out the gate, past Church and up the rise
toward Horn's Variety, that mythic place.
The path was new to me. I walked alone
and genuflected to inspect a sheared-
off branch, a mica fleck, a swallow's bone.
I used a stick to write *DAM HELL*, then cleared
away the words. Dust pleated in my skirt.
I felt a breath unloosen in my chest,
expanding, fearless in this wondrous dirt
of disobedience, this fresh unrest.
The church bells rang. I rose, denied the call.
Picked freedom, sin, a red hot Fireball.

Love Note

Unseen, she tucked it in her lover's coat
while he was busy packing up his clothes
and laptop for a week away. The note
might be discovered on the plane. Who knows?
Or still much later in a hotel room
before he settles into bed alone.
Alone. She feels a sudden sense of doom
about things left undone and things unknown.
What if the letter falls out like a glove,
lost in a crowded airport ticket line,
then stamped by ruthless heels that can't feel love?
She wishes she had sent a clearer sign—
concealed her words where only he could see,
tattooed beneath his skin, indelibly.

José Edmundo Ocampo Reyes

Portrait of Chichikov as a Mortgage Trader

> Acquisition is to blame for everything; because of it things
> have been done which the world dubs *not quite clean*.
> —Nikolai Gogol (trans., Pevear and Volokhonsky)

He buys up all the mortgages he can,
cramming their cash flows into CDOs
investors crave, though they don't understand
the risk of loss. Not even Moody's knows.
He buys up billions' worth but doesn't care
whose loans these are; what matters is his spread.
As they continue living, unaware,
to him these souls may just as well be dead.

Today a single name catches his eye:
Tatiana, waitress, sole support of four. . . .
But the next trade cuts short his reverie,
denying him a glimpse into her war—
the home, the bonds she fights in vain to save
while she becomes her labor, like a slave.

José Edmundo Ocampo Reyes

Instructions to Travelers from the Third World

Before you cross the border, you must learn how to use your passport,
the sine qua non of any voyage. Guard it as your life; you must not
    lose your passport.

Your photo may adorn it, but it really is the property of your
    crumbling republic,
as you are. It is a crime to alter or reproduce your passport.

Peculiar to you as your shadow, your fingerprint, your double helix,
it is neither carte blanche nor diary of hopes. Don't abuse your
    passport.

You dream of glimpsing snow, cathedrals, fist-sized diamonds
    plundered from your land. . . .
First you must queue for hours in the sun, wait for the consul to
    peruse your passport.

When he slams down his crimson stamp like a gavel, and you walk
    home,
dusting off your shame, how easy it will be to accuse your passport!

(But it is guiltless as a tortured root that causes you to trip and break
    a bone.
Blame instead your fellow terrorists and refugees, and excuse your
    passport.)

Think you can sneak by without a visa, feign ignorance, charm
the immigration officer
with your strange locution? Your scheme will boomerang once
he views your passport.

Your name, the theorems you've proved, your cancer cure are of
no consequence.
Its pages blighted fields, your passport is your world. You cannot
choose your passport.

Boondocks

> According to the *2002 Encyclopaedia Britannica Book of*
> *the Year*, the Philippines has the fourth-largest population
> of English speakers in the world, ranking after the United
> States, India, and the United Kingdom.

To show our appreciation for your gift
of language, we'd like to offer you one word
of our own, *bundók*, which means "mountain."

It may not slide as smoothly off your tongue
as the French *montagne*, but we hope nonetheless
your lexicon can accommodate this term,

which has been blessed by the goddess who scatters
ginger along Makiling's slopes. Keep it
as a souvenir of the times we fought side by side

when the Japanese hunted us down
in the Cordilleras, and let your poets repeat it
when they recount those still-unnamed battles

in their slim volumes. Remember to say the word
out loud, for luck, before you leave our shores,
your frigates full of timber, siblings, gold.

Marybeth Rua-Larsen

Spiderwort

I sit alone in your room, spinning all the things you touched
and wouldn't let go of. Sea stars and periwinkle shells
arranged and rearranged on your bureau, lotion smoothed
and pressed on the inside of your tiny wrists like perfume,
the reek of vanilla everywhere. Sometimes, you'd twirl
and twirl and twirl, believing dizzy made you strong.

Two floors below, spiderwort blooms,
casting its deep bruising purple everywhere
and I remember, in our first home, when I named it *weed*,
spent an entire summer dragging it up by its roots
worried it would overcome the dahlias;
but true wildflowers don't die, and I've grown

to love such intrepidness, watching each
three-petaled bloom close at sunset
while the next lies in wait for sunrise. Unstoppable,
like you, twirling, my arms outstretched
to catch you. Dangers lurk everywhere;
the worst we don't see coming.

Marybeth Rua-Larsen

West Second Street, Oswego, 1986

I remember the walk more
than the movie. *Your birthday,*
your choice, you'd said, and it was

a luxury to lock our front door behind us,
follow the sidewalk downtown.
We stopped first at the river,

watched the moon back-stitch its silver
through the surface while the carp,
those golden outsiders never intending

to stay, rolled beneath then rose,
open-mouthed, gaping like the family
we'd left behind. Every step past

the flickering marquee, its dim bulbs framing
Pretty in Pink, was ghost-lit, and creeping
to the farthest, darkest seats,

we whispered all through the movie—
how easily carp learn moving water,
how salt lingers on the tongue

waiting for relief. After the film arced
at the prom dress, all polka dots and bare
shoulders, the momentary spark

before it drifted away, we walked
home, passing a shadow of narcissus
in a stranger's garden. The moon hid

this time, fooled by a mask of clouds,
and with your arms around me, we paused, again,
at the river, listened as wave after small wave

spilled its troubles on the shore,
chanting *I won't let go, I won't let go,*
I won't let go.

Andrew Szilvasy

Faculty Welcome

She's like a tiger in a blizzard here
where olive oil is jade and where tomatoes
are colors other than tomatoes. Near
these heirlooms, she is struck by what can go
for salad: bulgur, chickpeas, mint, all stirred,
yet lacking lettuce. Thinking on the matter,
she knows the only fare that wouldn't faze
her father are the newly popped champagnes.

Her mother always told her that the work
would pay, the hours spent alone in dim lights.
But what did she know of the stress of fork
placements, the elements of elegance
lost on those born where few if any parks
display the name of local socialites?
And her peers assume the best of her, she fears,
because they only know her over beers.

She's smirked through many a male peer's lectures, bluffed
her love of Mondrian, and gently smiled
at Dad, who smoothly shepherds guests to his loved
Kinkade he bought online. She rationalizes
beforehand why she doesn't call enough,
and trains her face for her apology:
her family has long since had their fill
of hearing justifications and bull.

Yet they ask questions for appearance's sake;
they really want to care but are resigned
that when she speaks, they'll hardly stay awake.
She knows they find her less than genuine,
and so she's worked on it. She's tried to make
herself fit in—their interests don't align.
She doesn't get "the sports" and hates hot fashion;
in one ear Gronk, the other, a Kardashian.

Her home friends bore; she calls them still, but their
brief conversations rarely touch on substance:
it's mostly stories of a friend's friend's sister
who has three kids, no time, and who just once
would like if Tinder helped her land an affair.
Yet her work peers frustrate her: their insistence
on every moral failing only guilts her.
Why can't she just enjoy her hamburger?

This little campus gathering to celebrate
the appointment of a president offers
a guiltless night. She can have a cocktail
and not be asked to proffer thoughts on Chaucer.
She pours herself Prosecco, sits and waits
to see if anyone will bother with her.
She hopes they don't and takes a sip. It's cheap.
No shock: the school's financial outlook's bleak.

So she's alone beside *hors d'oeuvres*. Sure, her nights
are days: restless, lonely, shadows and gray tones.
No, her monograph's not near complete,
the midnight hours wasted. Is she dismayed? No.
She's slowly getting the hang of this. Besides,
she's waited a long time to taste tomatoes
that do not crumble, meal-like, on keen lips,
and drink these bubbles rising ever up.

Andrew Szilvasy

Beyond All Change

The earth is beautiful beyond all change.
I think it's the *all* that really gets me.
Naked trees in a milk-white field

or eagles picture-still on mountains
that cradle the jaws of late leviathans:
these are beautiful beyond all change.

And I can even see the deep-sea beauty
of the anglerfish, whose
take on love makes true the human lie:

flesh of our flesh, blood of our blood.
But is the poet right about *all* change?
There will come a time when the bloated

sun will drink the rocks
and breathe the oceans: when we sit
with crows in flaming trees,

will we walk hand-in-hand admiring
the mountains that melt around us?

Toni Treadway

All the Weird Ones Come to Me

because I look them in the eye
because my big brother is crazy
all the bag men, the artists, gonzos,
spare change rattling,
careful gleam-in-the-eye, nothing-up-the-sleeve,
hustle around so that no one sees,
quick-quick men—
all the fruitcakes you're bound to meet
on the streets of America

so I visit my brother in the nuthouse
and they gather around
to bum a light,
to smell me to tell me to show me
and never once to hurt me
except in their pressing-in all the time
with so much need

and then my brother shepherds me outside
to his own needs
more transparent to me than the ones inside

if I touch him as he leaves
he does not leave so hard nor go so far.

You in Socks

The shine on red oak stairs and you in socks:
"That's how I polish them," you say and laugh.
So, down you go—with water in a glass,
"Look, ma, no hands!"—to tumble on your ass.

Watch out, my love, do not upend your life
with urgent trips to doctors and PT.
Please understand. I'm sorry but it's me,
with worries brimming to the nth degree.

I have to let my would-be mother out.
Maternal energies, when set aside,
can turn into hovering by a spouse
who wants to tend her loved ones, lest they fall
into swift depths or be consumed by all
the dragons underneath her childless bed.

Toni Treadway

Overheard at the Grotto above Assisi

The hermit murmurs softly in his chamber.
His tears wet the narrow limestone walls.
A bright sleet falls on the mountain,
icy fog obscures the town.

Give dominion back to the creatures.
Let the cows give milk to their young
and the asses walk unburdened.
Let the birds fatten and flock.
May the dragonfly dry his glistening wings
and sunlight bless the bees on their rounds.

The Shawl

The fine old shawl I'm wearing
has dark patterns in the weaving
that give texture to my dreaming,
all handmade.

Is my weary search for meaning
or believing or becoming,
all my endless careful mending,
just charade?

Yet the fabric's growing stronger
while the wearer's getting weaker,
and the mender meets the weaver
unafraid.

Late Harvest

The berries that withstand the frost,
if they endure at all,
have liquored juice and puckered flesh
unlike the fruit of fall.

They're hanging in the garden's ruin
until some hand or wing
can part the crumpled, mildewed leaves,
and grasp the precious thing.

Paulette Demers Turco

Work or Play

What draws me to the soil in May?
When jonquils' yellow trumpets fade,
I wear loose clothes to dig all day.
I could be sipping lemonade.

Instead, I shape the yews with shears,
wear visored cap and cotton socks,
mix compost, loam and sweat salt tears.
I tear through roots and toss small rocks.

I choose my plants for shade or sun;
form tiers; mix textures, spans of bloom;
plant chives and basil just for fun,
French marigolds where I find room.

Memorial Day, my view, once plain,
is crowned by rainbows after rain.

Paulette Demers Turco

Almost Overnight in Tuam

1970s at St. Mary's Mother and Baby Home

They stumbled in a pile of baby bones
and skulls whose eyeless faces stared at them
as if remembering beyond the wall.
The two boys dropped the apple cores, ran home
so fast, their legs could hardly carry them.
Their story jumbled, mom and dad believed them,
warned them, "You boys, never go back! Never.
Never!" They couldn't help it. Something drew them—
maybe the sound of large equipment rumbling.
This change happened almost overnight?
The apple trees had vanished. Grass was laid,
the blue of Holy Mary's mantle glistening
in a grotto. Trace of cracked concrete,
hidden alabaster bones—all gone.

Singer

The last time mother closed her sewing machine,
she'd sewn my sister's gown of silk and lace,
a veil with pearls, fulfilling her own wish.
The house, now her own space, would have no hum.
She'd reached the private goal she'd set herself:
to dress each daughter till her wedding day . . .

plus bridesmaids' gowns and her own dress that day.
She'd learned how fabrics stressed her one machine,
and oiled it well, used threads she chose herself.
She learned the slip of silk, the weave of lace,
learned to guide her Singer, feel its hum—
with yards and yards of fabric toward her wish

of daughters dressed by her—beyond her wish
when she took her vows on her wedding day.
While her love served in Normandy, she'd hum
soft tunes of his return—no sewing machine.
Her trousseau was of borrowed silk and lace.
Her groom gave her a Singer. She'd teach herself.

She made her first dress simply, for herself—
an A-line shift in navy blue. Her wish,
for Christmas velvet, Easter's handmade lace,
came first in trimmings for each holiday.
As we arrived, she cherished her machine;
from birth, we breathed in rhythm with its hum.

She'd set the bobbin, press the footplate, hum
a favorite tune, and fit each dress herself
in pastels, flowered prints, as her machine
sewed ribbons, pleats—yes, every daughter's wish
for birthdays, dances, gowns for spring prom day—
velvet, chiffon, rayon, linen, lace.

All sewing done, she stored away her lace—
knit baby blankets. Names soon blurred. Her hums
for cherished lullabies, her once prized Wednesday
shopping trips, her pride and sense of self,
from outfits she'd designed—erased. Her wish
undone, she felt confusion: what machine,

what meal, what day, what daughter? What is lace?
Our photos proved how her machine did hum.
Our wish, her awe: *I stitched these gowns myself?*

Paulette Demers Turco

Hours Arrested

six months later

Again, Mom turns Dad's band on her right hand
and eyes the one with whom she shares the room.
Mom whispers, frowns, "But I don't understand.

How long has Dad been gone?" Her day's unplanned.
He'd be beside her, carving—memories loom
again. She turns his band on her right hand.

"Did I go to his wake?" Can she withstand
repeated jolts? She broods, "He was my groom,"
then whispers, frowns, "but I don't understand."

She nods, "I moved here once I lost him," and
her loss of time, his absence, fill the room.
She turns Dad's wedding band on her right hand

and glances at Dad's photos on the stand
beside her, near the jasmine lush with bloom.
She whispers, frowns, "But I don't understand."

The valentine she made for him by hand
fades on her memo board. The man for whom
she turns the band again on her right hand
is gone. She frowns, "But I don't understand."

Deborah Warren

Song of the Egg

If, when he looked, a prophet saw
inside the egg's imperfect O
a bantam little shadow—death
already curled in the heart of the embryo—

it would be too small a flaw
to brood on, if he heard as well,
clearer than light, a brilliant crowing
shatter the brittle confines of the shell.

Deborah Warren

Down-to-Earth

In the field the coyote yip-yips imminent danger;
    the dog in the kitchen rumbles a basso growl;
the field sends back a shrill elastic baying;
    the kitchen gives a soprano howl.

These two aren't discussing climate change,
    war, flu, layoffs; in this dialogue
a well-informed coyote's not relaying
    to a pessimistic dog

grounds for worry—national cases of mange,
    the mountain lion population swelling,
a cougar-sighting fifteen miles away—
    only a future close enough to smell.

Deborah Warren

Mole

Earth is his occupation, and the mole
works the turf in his native breaststroke, swimming
hallways into the sod—a geonaut
supreme, and connoisseur of worms; I've heard him
breaking roots an inch beneath my sole
and seen how the subterranean specialist
carves out for himself a single, simple role.
I envy the expertise he brings to bear
on dirt, the narrow office he was given;
as for me, my habitat is thought,
where I grope and sweat and scrabble out a living
forced to prove—up here in a windy lair
as invisible as the mole's—that there exists
an animal who can dig a hole in air.

Deborah Warren

Swimmer

He pauses where the oaks beside the street
grow down into a puddle, with the trees
towering so far below him that—
half-immersed in the landscape at his feet,
leaning over the surface-sheen—he sees
evidence that the earth is far from flat

and, diving into the two dimensions, swims
down, deeper, toward whatever breeze
stirs the branches and ruffles the buried sky,
flutter-kicking his way among the limbs
below: but the water won't give up the trees,
and he shakes himself and returns to the surface, dry.

Deborah Warren

Haircut

The stream of hair doesn't resist the scissors'
silver kiss and, here and there,
flashing under the rasps and hisses,
falls around the chair,

as if I'd cut the brilliant streak of ice
flying off a comet's tail—
taken giant shears and sliced
the evaporated hail,
brought the great blades down, and come inside
having severed light from light:

the broom's beside the door,
the job well done; I should be satisfied
to sweep the hair away despite
its brilliance on the floor.

Un bar aux Folies-Bergère

(after Édouard Manet)

Let me describe an accident I had
where I fell suddenly into two dimensions:
I was standing at the kitchen table
thinking about my winter jacket, maybe,
maybe about the Black Death, or the dog;
my arms isosceles to the table's surface,
hands, on both sides, out along its edge—
I'm someone else! a trick of recognition,
and in a flash my body is transposed

into the barmaid *aux* Folies-Bergère.
I'm there. I've been assumed into the picture
where I've taken flesh among the bottles,
hands on the marble bar, and in the mirrors
the chandelier, the smoky room, *buveurs*;
the velvet ribbon around my throat, the locket;
and under the rose in my décolletage,
I'm corseted into a serious hourglass.
There'll be heartburn before the night is out.

It's a painting. It's flat. Pick at the surface;
no way in—there's no *z*-axis. But
I'm there, in Paris, 1880-something.
Another time—a couch and a cushion—I'm
Maja desnuda. Or yearning across a field,
I'm *Christina*. Back into three dimensions,
I'm *The Thinker*. I'm *Discobolus*.
I just pick up the pose and run with it
like Proteus escaping from himself.

Deborah Warren

The Ballet of the Eight-Week Kittens

With such abandon—buoyant wide *jetés*
around the kitchen, furniture, and air
possessed by arcs of fur and ricochets,
plunges and cabrioles—they're everywhere.
Dance, kittens. Take the table, flying
jump-drunk: You have cause to pirouette,
more than you dream of—barns and meadows lying
outside—things you don't imagine yet.
Hurl yourselves in knots across the floor;
leaps, demented *entrechats*. Ignore
the galaxies beyond the kitchen door.
And, when you tumble to it that there's *more*
than this—more than the little world you know—
take me out there with you when you go.

Jay Wickersham

Blackout (1965)

We're playing Monopoly by candlelight.
My mother rolls a six; she goes to jail.
I throw down cash, erect a red hotel
On Park Place. New York is full of night.
Darkness drifts in through the apartment windows.
The buildings stand around, dim and far-
Away as fathers. We play a little more.
The silence grows too big; we haul our pillows
And blankets into the living room, make side-by-side
Nests with sofa cushions on the floor.
Hours later the lights shock us out of sleep.
Blinking, we meet the many-windowed stare
Of the city. Slowly it subsides
To blackness—but less private now, less deep.

Jay Wickersham

Two Scenes after Edward Hopper

Alone is never lonely. Anyone
Who ever woke to empty city streets
Knows this. Your knees make mountains of the sheets;
The curtains waver outward, toward the sun-
Touched fronts of buildings. Now your eyes align
Each window. Is it just a painted set,
A backdrop to your waking? Stand erect;
Abrade your dreaming skin on brick and stone.

Alone is often lonely. In dark woods
A line of globes glows red and white above
The gas pumps. Like milk in water, light
Seeps out into the darkness, staining the night
With longing. But now you slam the hood,
Restart your car. The road begins to move.

Jay Wickersham

The Stain on the Ceiling

Under the paint slapped on by the last owner
It waits, smiles faintly, listening
    To your plans:
These blank walls will give no scope
To disappointment; here your schemes won't fail
    Or go aslant.

Deferential as a movie butler
It quietly appears, a small brown spot,
    One rainy day,
Almost small enough to be a spider,
Almost faint enough to be a dirt smudge,
    Easily wiped away.

But it's not wiped away. Like a bat, it slumbers
On the ceiling, seeming to grow a little
    Every night.
You move softly, hoping it won't awaken,
Look about, unfold its webbed brown wings
    Across your sight.

The rain betrays you. Breathing moistly,
The stain reshapes itself, bubbling brown smoke
    In which you see
Faces become ghosts, great cities built
And burned, enchanted isles dissolving
    In the sea.

Dry weather brings relief. The sky turns blue
And hard, seals up your fears inside
    A watertight skin.
Better to burn in a Saharan world
Than suffer such damp insinuations.
    You call in

Roofers, masons, plasterers, painters
To purge your past, undo the sins that ache
    With every rain.
But no matter how you try to mend the surface,
    There's still a stain.

Jay Wickersham

Night Crossing

Midnight. My son sprawls
In the tangle of his sheets.
Below, his general
Measures cannon shots

Toward a cliff of piled-up books.
Across the wood-grain river
A bridge spans toward the city.
We walk across together,

My son and I. The walls
And towers loom above.
We see a toppled arch,
A house without a roof,

The castle where the king
And court are hatching schemes,
Where history proceeds
And prisoners have names.

I feel his anxious grip,
The press of finger bone.
Some day I'll have to stop
While he goes on alone.

Anton Yakovlev

Peter's Denial

We turned our backs on you that very day,
too frightened to bear witness in your trial.
Now your small motorboat, sunk in the bay,
haunts the horizon.
      They had no file
on you, so they came up with some BS.
Some lazy fingers chicken-scratched your crime.
The firing squad wasn't on hand, I guess,
so they reduced your sentence to hard time.

Your room stands vacant. Your half-open door
keeps pummeling your out-of-tune guitar,
echoing in the downstairs taffy store.

Your phone, incinerated with your car,
dials us every night at half past four
to let us know exactly what we are.

Anton Yakovlev

The Informant

The man in the vest adjusted his hair.
His eyes were electric blue.
You knew who he was and why he was there.
Sadly, no one else knew.

Then Boris came out with his Trotsky quip,
said Trotsky wasn't that bad.
You noticed the blue-eyed man bite his lip.
Nothing more would need to be said.

You watched it unfold for the rest of the night:
the way Boris kept getting lit,
the charm he turned on, his teammates' delight
at his escapist wit.

The next morning you knew not to look for him.
His room was empty and clean.
The hotel had checked in no one by that name.
He was never heard from again.

It's been decades. Your children are teaching school.
Last December, the Curtain fell.
Some teammates of yours fell to alcohol.
You're retired, still in decent health.

You think of Boris, that talking dead
on that night of pickles and vodka,
and the shadow of Asrael over his head
in the shape of a blue-eyed informant.

Was he sent to the Gulag, or was he shot
in the head right there in the yard?
You will never switch off this thought.
You will never get a fresh start.

There are bullet holes in the back of the bus
and behind the old kindergarten.
There is blood in the benches where fathers drink kvass
and ex-convicts make concept art.

You walk these streets every single day.
You drive your Jeep among ghosts.
You've grown accustomed to it. It's okay.
Nothing revealed, nothing lost.

Only sometimes, at home, you let out a sigh.
Your granddaughter looks up at you.
You notice her look, raise an eyebrow, smile.
Her eyes are electric blue.

Anton Yakovlev

Ask Anyone

Ask anyone who lived in Soviet times.
It was at night that people went away.
Faint blood in basements. Vague rumors of crimes.
Ask anyone who lived in Soviet times.
Quiet black Volgas gliding past stop signs.
Limbs sticking out of trucks at break of day.
Ask anyone who lived in Soviet times.
It was at night that people went away.

Hepburn to Tracy: A Dismantling

I say goodbye to lamps, to figurines,
to the porch door you never left unlocked,
to your insomnia and to your dreams,
and to the horsehair chair in which you rocked.
For twenty-seven years you lived with me
in this small house. And it's been twenty more
since you got up that night to drink your tea
and fell face forward on the kitchen floor.

I'll miss our windows and our nothing view.
You know, dear Spence, I've changed my laugh for you.
Not that I hear it much, now you're away.
I'll keep your sense of humor, your ennui,
your books, your gateleg table, and—I pray—
that quiet way you sometimes looked at me.

About the Editor

PAULETTE DEMERS TURCO began writing verse when she learned she soon would be a grandmother. She took Rhina P. Espaillat's Lyceum poetry course and joined Alfred Nicol's poetry workshop. Her poetry has appeared in the *Lyric, Ibbetson Street,* the Sonnet Scroll feature of the *Poetry Porch, Merrimac Mic Anthologies* (II–V), *Poems for Plovers* (Hawk & Whippoorwill, 2020), and the *2020 Hippocrates Awards Anthology.* In 2018, Finishing Line Press published her chapbook, *In Silence,* and she became a member of the Powow River Poets. She co-organizes Powow bimonthly poetry readings. Her awards include the Robert Frost Poetry Award; commendation in the FPM-Hippocrates Health Professional Prize for Poetry and Medicine; first prize in the Rockport Ekphrastic Poetry Contest; and an MFA in Writing President's Award at Lesley University, Cambridge, Massachusetts. She earned her MFA in writing from Lesley University in 2019 and in the same year, also retired from academic and clinical optometry. She lives in Newburyport, Massachusetts.

Contributors

MEREDITH BERGMANN is a sculptor whose public monuments can be seen in Boston, Massachusetts, and New York, New York. Her publications include *Barrow Street, Contemporary Poetry Review*, the *Hopkins Review*, the *Hudson Review, Light, Mezzo Cammin*, the *New Criterion, Raintown Review, TriQuarterly Review*; and the anthologies *Hot Sonnets* (Entasis Press, 2011), *Love Affairs at the Villa Nelle* (Kelsay Books, 2018), and *Alongside We Travel: Contemporary Poets on Autism* (New York Quarterly Books, 2019). She was poetry editor of *American Arts Quarterly* from 2006–2017. Her chapbook, *A Special Education*, was published in 2014 by EXOT Books.

WENDY CANNELLA's poetry has appeared in *Balancing Act 2: An Anthology of Poems by Fifty Maine Women* (Littoral Books, 2018), *Crab Creek Review* (Poetry Prize semifinalist), *Mid-American Review, Mom Egg Review, Painted Bride Quarterly, RHINO, Salamander, Solstice*, and others. Her essay "Angels and Terrorists" is featured in *The Room and the World: Essays on the Poet Stephen Dunn* (Syracuse University Press, 2013). Coeditor of the anthology *Lunation* (Senile Monk Press, 2019), Cannella served as co-chair for the Portsmouth Poet Laureate Project board of directors, and was a Maine Literary Award finalist. She lives in York Harbor, Maine.

MICHAEL CANTOR's second full length collection is *Furusato* (Kelsay Books, 2019); his first is *Life in the Second Circle* (Able Muse Press, 2012), a finalist for the Able Muse Book Award and the Massachusetts Book Award for Poetry. His chapbook, *The Performer* (Pudding House Publications, 2007), was his first published collection. His work has appeared in the *Dark Horse, Measure, Raintown Review, Frogpond, New Walk, THINK, Light*, and numerous other journals and anthologies. A native New Yorker, he has lived and worked in Japan, Latin America, and Europe. He presently divides his time between Plum Island, Massachusetts, and Santa Fe, New Mexico.

BARBARA LYDECKER CRANE is a two-time finalist for the Rattle Poetry Prize, a two-time winner of the Laureates' Choice prize from the Maria W. Faust Sonnet Contest, and a first prize winner in the Helen Schaible International Sonnet Contest. She has published three chapbooks: *BackWords Logic* (Local Gems Press, 2017), *Alphabetricks* (Daffydowndilly Press, 2013), and *Zero Gravitas* (White Violet Press, 2012). Her poems have appeared in *First Things, Light, Measure, THINK,* the *Writer's Almanac,* and several anthologies. Crane is also an artist. She finds it enticing to often write from another's viewpoint, and thoroughly enjoys writing in both light and serious styles (and sometimes somewhere in between).

ROBERT W. CRAWFORD has published two books of poetry, *The Empty Chair* (University of Evansville Press, 2012), winner of the Richard Wilbur Poetry Award, and *Too Much Explanation Can Ruin a Man* (WordTech Communications, 2005). He is a two-time winner of the Howard Nemerov Sonnet Award. He is a longtime member of the Powow River Poets. Currently, he is the Director of Frost Farm Poetry in Derry, New Hampshire, which includes the Hyla Brook Reading Series, the Frost Farm Poetry Conference, and the Frost Farm Poetry Prize. He was named the first Poet Laureate of Derry, New Hampshire, in January 2017. He lives in Chester, New Hampshire, with his wife, the poet Midge Goldberg.

DAVID DAVIS has been a member of the Powow River Poets since 2005. He served as the Poet-in-Residence at the Joppa Flats Massachusetts Audubon Center for four years and has been a volunteer at Joppa Flats since 2003. He has published four books, all from Bard Brook Press: *Market Town and Other Poems* (2020), *The Joy Poems* (2018), *Joppa Flats* (2017), and *Crossing Streams on Rocks* (2011). He has a varied professional background, having worked as a surveyor, special ed teacher, peace corps volunteer in Morocco, philosophy professor, artificial intelligence researcher, and high-tech entrepreneur.[†]

M. FROST DELANEY is a bean counter by trade, a tree hugger in heart, and a recovering soul, who practices life in New England.

---

† Having been fully engaged in the copyediting of his contributions to this anthology all the way to completion, David Davis, sadly, passed away July 11, 2020, just weeks before the book's prerelease, after a long battle with cancer.

RHINA P. ESPAILLAT has published twelve full-length books and five chapbooks, most recently two poetry collections titled *And After All* (Able Muse Press, 2019) and *The Field* (David Robert Books, 2019). Her work, which comprises poetry, essays, and short stories in both English and her native Spanish, and translations from and into both languages, appears in numerous journals, anthologies, and websites. She has received many national and international awards, including the Richard Wilbur Poetry Award, two Howard Nemerov Sonnet Awards, the T. S. Eliot Prize; several annual awards from the New England Poetry Club, the Poetry Society of America, and the Frost Foundation; various honors from the Dominican Republic's Ministry of Culture; and a Lifetime Achievement in the Arts Award from Salem State College. A founding member of the Melopoeia trio, Espaillat performs with poet Alfred Nicol and guitarist John Tavano, as well as with the quintet known as the Diminished Prophets, which includes vocalist Kate Sullivan and cellist Roger Kimball.

MIDGE GOLDBERG is winner of the Richard Wilbur Award and the New Hampshire Literary Awards Reader's Choice Award for her book *Snowman's Code* (University of Evansville Press, 2016). She has received the Howard Nemerov Sonnet Award. Her poems have appeared in many journals and anthologies, including *Poetry Speaks: Who I Am* and the *Writer's Almanac*. Her other books include *Flume Ride* (David Robert Books, 2006), and the children's book *My Best Ever Grandpa*, Valori Herzlich, illustrator (Azro Press, 2015). Goldberg is a longtime member of the Powow River Poets and has an MFA from the University of New Hampshire. She lives in Chester, New Hampshire, with her family, two cats, and an ever-changing number of chickens.

OWEN GREY is an English teacher and poet. He has been a member of the Powow River Poets since 2012. He lives in Cambridge, Massachusetts.

A.M. JUSTER's tenth book of original and translated poetry, *Wonder and Wrath*, will be published by Paul Dry Books in fall 2020. He is the only three-time winner of the Howard Nemerov Sonnet Award. He has won the Willis Barnstone Translation Prize and the Richard Wilbur Poetry Award, among many other literary awards. He has won awards for his work in healthcare and disability policy, including the national Alzheimer's Association's Humanitarian of the Year.

DON KIMBALL is the author of three chapbooks: *Tumbling* (Finishing Line Press, 2016), *Journal of a Flatlander* (Finishing Line Press, 2009), and *Skipping Stones* (Pudding House Publications, 2008). His poetry has appeared in the *Blue Unicorn*, the *Lyric*, *Rattle*, and various other journals and anthologies. Kimball is a longstanding member and the current moderator of the Powow River Poets, and in his third term as president of the Poetry Society of New Hampshire.

JOAN ALICE WOOD KIMBALL of Concord, Massachusetts, runs poetry workshops in Concord and Wayland, Massachusetts. Her latest poetry collection is *Early Light* (Kelsay Books, 2019). She has authored two illustrated poetry chapbooks, *Summer River* (Riverwood Books, 2013) and *This River Hill* (Blurb, 2009), and coedited a third. She was a finalist for the Morton Marr Poetry Prize and three *Atlanta Review* poetry prizes. She performed with the poetry troupe X.J. Kennedy & the Light Brigade on stage, TV, and at four Massachusetts Poetry Festivals. Her poetry has appeared in *Measure, Raintown Review, Arion*, the *Comstock Review, Peacock Journal*, and many other journals. Her limerick, "Cold October," is inscribed on granite in Edmands Park, Newton, Massachusetts.

JEAN L. KREILING is a Professor of Music at Bridgewater State University in Massachusetts; she previously taught English at Western Carolina University in North Carolina. She has authored two full-length poetry collections: *Arts & Letters & Love* (Kelsay Books, 2018) and *The Truth in Dissonance* (Kelsay Books, 2014). She is the winner of several prizes, including the Plymouth Poetry Contest, the Kelsay Books Metrical Poetry Contest, three New England Poetry Club prizes, the Laureates' Choice prize in the Maria W. Faust Sonnet Contest, the Great Lakes Commonwealth of Letters Sonnet Award, the String Poet Prize, and the Able Muse Write Prize for Poetry.

NANCY BAILEY MILLER, a Powow River Poet for over twenty years, has published six books of poems—most recently, *Tacking Lessons* (The Cheshire Press, 2016). Her prose book *Of Minitmen & Molly's* (Tabby House, 2002) is a collection of stand-alone articles she wrote for the Town Crossings column of the *Lawrence Eagle Tribune*. Her poetry has appeared in the anthologies *The Crafty Poet* (Wind Publications, 2013), *The 2010 Poets' Guide to New Hampshire: More Places, More Poets* (Poetry Society of New Hampshire, 2009), *The Powow River Anthology* (Ocean Press, 2006), and *Merrimack Poetry Anthology* (Loom Press, 1992). Her poetry has also appeared in several journals, including *Rattapallax, Fine Lines, Blue Unicorn, Quill & Parchment*, the Sonnet Scroll feature of the *Poetry Porch*, and *Lighten Up Online*. Miller taught writing at Phillips Academy Andover for eleven summers. In addition to writing, Miller loves playing string quartets and racing sailboats in Marblehead, Massachusetts.

ANNE MULVEY began writing poetry in response to her brother Michael's death in 1994. Since then she has incorporated poetry and creative writing into her teaching and has led creative writing workshops for teens and elders in Lowell. Mulvey is a Professor Emerita of Psychology at the University of Massachusetts Lowell, an Amherst Writers and Artists Leader, and a longtime member of the Powows.

JAMES NAJARIAN grew up on a goat farm in Berks County, Pennsylvania. He teaches nineteenth-century British literature at Boston College, where he edits the journal *Religion and the Arts*. He is the author of *The Goat Songs* (University of North Texas Press, 2018), winner of the Vassar Miller Prize in Poetry.

ALFRED NICOL's most recent full-length collection of poetry is *Animal Psalms* (Able Muse Press, 2016). He has published two other collections, *Elegy for Everyone* (Prospero's World Press, 2010), and *Winter Light* (University of Evansville Press, 2004), winner of the Richard Wilbur Poetry Award. Nicol has collaborated with Rhina Espaillat and artist Kate Sullivan to create the chapbook *Brief Accident of Light* (Kelsay Books, 2019); and with his sister, the artist Elise Nicol, to create *Second Hand Second Mind* (Blurb, 2011). He edited *The Powow River Anthology* (Ocean Press, 2006). His poems have appeared in *Poetry*, the *New England Review*, the *Dark Horse, First Things, Commonweal*, the *Formalist*, the *Hopkins Review, Measure*, and many other journals and anthologies.

KYLE POTVIN's chapbook, *Sound Travels on Water* (Finishing Line Press, 2012), won the Jean Pedrick Chapbook Award. She is a two-time finalist for the Howard Nemerov Sonnet Award. Her poems have appeared in *Bellevue Literary Review, Crab Creek Review, Tar River Poetry*, the *New York Times, JAMA*, and others. She is an advisor to Frost Farm Poetry in Derry, New Hampshire, and for the last five years, has helped produce the New Hampshire Poetry Festival. Her full-length poetry collection, *Loosen*, is forthcoming from Hobblebush Books in January 2021. Potvin lives with her husband and two sons in Derry, New Hampshire.

José Edmundo Ocampo Reyes, born and raised in the Philippines, is the author of the chapbook *Present Values* (Backbone Press, 2018), winner of the Jean Pedrick Chapbook Award from the New England Poetry Club. His poems have appeared in various Philippine and US journals and have been anthologized in *No Tender Fences: An Anthology of Immigrant and First-Generation American Poetry* (2019); *The Achieve of, the Mastery: Filipino Poetry and Verse from English, Mid-'90s to 2016* (University of the Philippines Press, 2018); *Villanelles* (Everyman's Library, 2012); and *The Powow River Anthology* (Ocean Publishing, 2006).

Marybeth Rua-Larsen lives on the south coast of Massachusetts. Her poems have appeared in *Orbis*, *Crannóg*, the *Cape Cod Poetry Review*, *Cleaver*, *Measure*, and *American Arts Quarterly*, among other journals. She has received a Hawthornden Fellowship; the Luso-American Fellowship for the DISQUIET International Literary Program; the Galway Kinnell Poetry Prize; and the Parent-Writer Fellowship in Poetry from the Martha's Vineyard Institute of Creative Writing. She has been awarded the Over the Edge New Writer of the Year in Poetry. Her chapbook *Nothing In-Between* was published by Barefoot Muse Press in 2014.

Andrew Szilvasy teaches British literature outside of Boston, Massachusetts. His poems have appeared in *CutBank, Barrow Street, Smartish Pace, Tar River Poetry*, the *American Journal of Poetry*, and *RHINO*, among others. He lives in Boston with his wife.

Toni Treadway, after viewing a members' show at the Newburyport Art Association, bought two books, both titled *Greatest Hits* (Pudding House Publications, 2003): one was by David Berman and the second by Rhina P. Espaillat, both of them members of the Powow River Poets, a working group that gave monthly readings at the NAA. Espaillat invited Treadway to attend workshops and poetry became reintegrated into her life. She has co-organized the Powow poetry readings since 2015. The title poem of her book, *Late Harvest* (Kelsay Books, 2018), was runner-up for the Robert Frost Poetry Award. She works with Bob Brodsky to restore old movie film for public television and archives.

Paulette Demers Turco: see page 136.

DEBORAH WARREN's poetry has appeared in the *New Yorker*, the *Paris Review*, *Poetry*, and the *Yale Review*. Her books include *Connoisseurs of Worms* and *Etymo! Etymology for Serious Entertainment*, both forthcoming from Paul Dry Books in 2021; the translation *Ausonius: The Moselle and Other Poems* (Routledge, 2017); *Dream with Flowers and Bowl of Fruit* (University of Evansville Press, 2008), winner of the Richard Wilbur Poetry Award; *Zero Meridian* (Ivan R. Dee, 2004), winner of the New Criterion Poetry Prize; and *The Size of Happiness* (Waywiser Press, 2003). Her other awards include the ALSCW Meringoff Prize, the Robert Frost Poetry Award, the Howard Nemerov Sonnet Award, and the Robert Penn Warren Prize.

JAY WICKERSHAM's poems and essays have appeared in, among others, *Agni*, the *Formalist*, the *High Window*, the *Poetry Porch*, the *William & Mary Review*, and the *Harvard Review* (an essay on having Seamus Heaney as a teacher). He was a finalist for the Howard Nemerov Sonnet Award. Wickersham lives in Cambridge, Massachusetts, where he practices environmental and architectural law.

ANTON YAKOVLEV's latest chapbook is *Chronos Dines Alone* (SurVision Books, 2018), winner of the James Tate Prize. *The Last Poet of the Village* (Sensitive Skin Books, 2019) is a book of Yakovlev's translations of poetry by Sergei Yesenin. Yakovlev is also the author of *Ordinary Impalers* (Kelsay Books, 2017) and two prior chapbooks: *The Ghost of Grant Wood* (Finishing Line Press, 2015) and *Neptune Court* (The Operating System, 2015). His poems have appeared in the *New Yorker*, the *Hopkins Review*, *Amarillo Bay*, *Measure*, and elsewhere. Originally from Moscow, Russia, Anton is a graduate of Harvard University and the education director at the Bowery Poetry Club.

Acknowledgments

MEREDITH BERGMANN: "The Bird in the Bathroom" first appeared in the *Hudson Review*. The poem "Period Furniture: The Royal Bedchamber" is from the series "Period Furniture," set in an imaginary museum. Poems are reprinted by permission of the poet.

DAVID BERMAN: "The Effect of Hearing the Sublime" first appeared in *Peacock Journal*. Poem is reprinted by permission of the poet's estate.

WENDY CANNELLA: "The Word *Slut*" first appeared in *Balancing Act 2: An Anthology of Poems by Fifty Maine Women* (Littoral Books, 2018). Poems are reprinted by permission of the poet.

MICHAEL CANTOR: "Tree Swallows in August" first appeared in *14 by 14*, "The Love of Sushi Sue" in *Soundzine*, "To an Old Friend Who Died Young" in *Lucid Rhythms*, and "Lament" in *Shit Creek Review*. These poems were reprinted in *Furusato* (Kelsay Books, 2019). "For Harry, Who Had Three Passports" first appeared in *Margie* and was reprinted in *Life in the Second Circle* (Able Muse Press, 2012). Poems are reprinted by permission of the poet.

BARBARA LYDECKER CRANE: "My Fault Lines" first appeared in *Light*. "Conjuring a Son" first appeared in *Zero Gravitas* (White Violet Press, 2012), was featured in the *Writer's Almanac*, and was reprinted in the anthology *Forgetting Home: Poems about Alzheimer's* (Barefoot Muse Press, 2013). "Shards of Knowing" first appeared in *Measure*. Poems are reprinted by permission of the poet.

Robert W. Crawford: "The Empty Chair" first appeared in *Measure* and was reprinted in *The Empty Chair* (University of Evansville Press, 2012), winner of the Richard Wilbur Poetry Award. "A Passenger" first appeared in the *Evansville Review* and "Hawks in the Leaves" in *First Things*. Poems are reprinted by permission of the poet.

David Davis: "Sonnet with Horse," "Larkspur," "The Waterfall," "The Juggler," and "Dawn" first appeared in *Crossing Streams on Rocks* (Bard Brook Press, 2011). Poems are reprinted by permission of the poet.

M. Frost Delaney: Poems are printed by permission of the poet.

Rhina P. Espaillat: "After" first appeared in *And After All* (Able Muse Press, 2019). "Just Stopping" first appeared in *Light* and was reprinted in *The Field* (David Robert Books, 2019). "On the Promenade" first appeared in *Brief Accident of Light: Poems of Newburyport* (Kelsay Books, 2019). "Bra," a semifinalist for the Emily Dickinson Award, first appeared in *PoemTree. com* and was reprinted in *Where Horizons Go* (Truman State University Press, 1998), winner of the T. S. Eliot Prize. "Guidelines" first appeared in *Her Place in These Designs* (Truman State University Press, 2008). Poems are reprinted by permission of the poet.

Midge Goldberg: "Walking on Ice" first appeared in *Mezzo Cammin* and was reprinted in *Flume Ride* (David Robert Books, 2006) and *The 2008 Poets' Guide to New Hampshire* (Poetry Society of New Hampshire, 2008). "Snowman's Code," "At the U-Pick," and "Breakfast Shift at the Inn" first appeared in *Snowman's Code* (University of Evansville Press, 2016). "Paper Town" first appeared in *First Things* and "Telling" in *Able Muse*, and both were reprinted in *Snowman's Code*. Poems are reprinted by permission of the poet.

Owen Grey: Poems are printed by permission of the poet.

A.M. Juster: "Backup Plan" first appeared in *Light* and was reprinted with "Proposed Clichés" in *Sleaze and Slander* (Measure Press, 2016). "Love Song" first appeared in the *Evansville Review* and was reprinted in *The Billy Collins Experience* (Kelsay Books, 2016). "Houseguests" first appeared in the *Barefoot Muse* and was reprinted in *Sleaze and Slander*. "Fugitive Son" first appeared in the *Formalist* and was reprinted in *The Secret Language of Women* (University of Evansville Press, 2003). Poems are reprinted by permission of the poet.

DON KIMBALL: "William, 1949–1966" first appeared in the *Lyric*, "Journal of a Flatlander" in *Ship of Fools*, and "Birch" in *Iambs & Trochees*, and all were reprinted in *Journal of a Flatlander* (Finishing Line Press, 2009). "Birch" was also reprinted in *The 2008 Poets' Guide to New Hampshire* (Poetry Society of New Hampshire, 2008) and *The 2010 Poets' Guide to New Hampshire: More Places, More Poets* (Poetry Society of New Hampshire, 2009). "Burial for a Stray" first appeared in *Rattle*, was nominated for a Pushcart Prize, and was reprinted in *Tumbling* (Finishing Line Press, 2016). Poems are reprinted by permission of the poet.

JOAN ALICE WOOD KIMBALL: "On First Looking at Rembrandt's *The Shipbuilder and His Wife*" first appeared in *California Quarterly*. "Hypatia" first appeared in *Arion*: Maria Dzielska's *Hypatia of Alexandria* (Harvard University Press, 1995) includes letters of Hypatia's student, Synesius. "Chauvet Cave" first appeared in *Thema*: two associated images are at donsmaps.com/images/lion.jpg and uk.phaidon.com/agenda/art/picture-galleries/2011/march/10/inside-the-cave-of-forgotten-dreams/. "Rhymes from a River" first appeared in *Measure*. Poems are reprinted by permission of the poet.

JEAN L. KREILING: "Winter Boats" first appeared in the *Cannon's Mouth*, "No Escape" in *Off the Coast*, and both were reprinted in *The Truth in Dissonance* (Kelsay Books, 2014). "Left Out" first appeared in *Fresh Ink*. "Ovillejo for the Librarian" first appeared in *Antiphon* and was reprinted in *The Truth in Dissonance*. "Brahms on Interstate 95" first appeared in *Mezzo Cammin* and "*Children Playing on the Beach*" in *THINK*, and both were reprinted in *Arts & Letters & Love* (Kelsay Books, 2018). Poems are reprinted by permission of the poet.

NANCY BAILEY MILLER: "Suitcase" first appeared in *Risking Rallentando* (Fermata Books, 2008) and was reprinted in *Cradle Songs: An Anthology of Poems on Motherhood* (Sharmagne Leland-St. John, editor, 2010), winner of the International Book Award. "Eden 1843" first appeared in *Before the Dove Returns* (Strathmoor Books, 2004). Poems are reprinted by permission of the poet.

ANNE MULVEY: Poems are printed by permission of the poet.

JAMES NAJARIAN: "Genealogy" first appeared in *Boston College Magazine*, "The Frat Boys" in *Literary Imagination*, and both were reprinted in *The Goat Songs* (University of North Texas Press, 2018), winner of the Vassar Miller Prize in Poetry. "The Annunciation" first appeared in the *Mennonite*. Poems are reprinted by permission of the poet.

ALFRED NICOL: "One Day" first appeared in the *San Diego Reader* and was reprinted in *Animal Psalms* (Able Muse Press, 2016). "Old Haunt" first appeared in *Poetry* and was reprinted in *Elegy for Everyone* (Prospero's World Press, 2010). "October 1962" and "Nuts" first appeared in *Animal Psalms*. "At Dusk" first appeared in *Better Than Starbucks!* and was reprinted in *Brief Accident of Light* (Kelsay Books, 2019). Poems are reprinted by permission of the poet.

KYLE POTVIN: "Diagnosis" first appeared in the *American Journal of Poetry* (as "Abecedarian: Diagnosis"), "The Hard Work of Dying" in *The 2019 Hippocrates Prize Anthology* (Hippocrates Press, 2019), "To My Children Reading My Poetry after I'm Gone" in *Able Muse*, and "Fireball" in *Ecotone*. "Love Note," a finalist for the Howard Nemerov Sonnet Award, first appeared in *Measure*, was reprinted in *Sound Travels on Water* (Finishing Line Press, 2012). Poems are reprinted by permission of the poet.

JOSÉ EDMUNDO OCAMPO REYES: "Portrait of Chichikov as a Mortgage Trader" first appeared in *Crab Orchard Review*, "Instructions to Travelers from the Third World" in *Pleiades*, and "Boondocks" in *Michigan Quarterly Review*, and all were reprinted in *Present Values* (Backbone Press, 2018). Poems are reprinted by permission of the poet.

MARYBETH RUA-LARSEN: "Spiderwort" was nominated for Best of the Net Award and "West Second Street, Oswego, 1986" won the Galway Kinnell Poetry Contest. Both poems first appeared in *Autumn Sky Poetry Daily*. Poems are reprinted by permission of the poet.

ANDREW SZILVASY: "Faculty Welcome" first appeared in *THINK*. "Beyond All Change," with line one from William Bronk's "Midsummer," first appeared in *Loch Raven Review*. Poems are reprinted by permission of the poet.

Toni Treadway: "All the Weird Ones Come to Me" first appeared in the *Poetry Porch*, "The Shawl" in the *Lyric*, and both were reprinted in *Late Harvest* (Kelsey Books, 2018) along with "You in Socks," "Overheard at the Grotto above Assisi," and "Late Harvest," which was a runner-up for the Robert Frost Poetry Award. Poems are reprinted by permission of the poet.

Paulette Demers Turco: "Work or Play" first appeared in the *Lyric* and was reprinted in *In Silence* (Finishing Line Press, 2018). "Almost Overnight in Tuam" (the second sonnet from "Hidden Stains," a sonnet crown about the maternity home, which operated from 1925–1961) first appeared in *Ibbetson Street*. "Singer," winner of the Robert Frost Poetry Award, and "Hours Arrested" first appeared in *In Silence*. Poems are reprinted by permission of the poet.

Deborah Warren: "Song of the Egg" first appeared in *Poetry* and was reprinted in *Dream with Flowers and Bowl of Fruit* (University of Evansville Press, 2008). "Down-to-Earth" first appeared in *Literary Matters*, "Mole" in *Mezzo Cammin*, "*Un bar aux Folies-Bergère*" in the *Hudson Review*, and the three poems are forthcoming in *Connoisseur of Worms* (Paul Dry Books, 2021). "Swimmer" first appeared in *Dream with Flowers and Bowl of Fruit* and "Haircut" in the *Hudson Review*. "The Ballet of the Eight-Week Kittens" first appeared in *Swallow Anthology* and was reprinted in *Dream with Flowers and Bowl of Fruit*. Poems are reprinted by permission of the poet.

Jay Wickersham: "Blackout (1965)," "Two Scenes after Edward Hopper," and "The Stain on the Ceiling" first appeared in the *Formalist*. "Night Crossing" first appeared in *Vita Brevis*. Poems are reprinted by permission of the poet.

Anton Yakovlev: "Peter's Denial" first appeared in *Measure*, "The Informant" in the *New Criterion*, "Ask Anyone" in *Breadcrumbs*, and "Hepburn to Tracy: A Dismantling" in the *Rutherford Red Wheelbarrow*. Poems are reprinted by permission of the poet.

ALSO FROM ABLE MUSE PRESS

Jacob M. Appel, *The Cynic in Extremis – Poems*

William Baer, *Times Square and Other Stories;*
New Jersey Noir – A Novel;
New Jersey Noir (Cape May) – A Novel;

Lee Harlin Bahan, *A Year of Mourning (Petrarch) – Translation*

Melissa Balmain, *Walking in on People (Able Muse Book Award for Poetry)*

Ben Berman, *Strange Borderlands – Poems;*
Figuring in the Figure – Poems

David Berman, *Progressions of the Mind – Poems*

Lorna Knowles Blake, *Green Hill (Able Muse Book Award for Poetry)*

Michael Cantor, *Life in the Second Circle – Poems*

Catherine Chandler, *Lines of Flight – Poems*

William Conelly, *Uncontested Grounds – Poems*

Maryann Corbett, *Credo for the Checkout Line in Winter – Poems;*
Street View – Poems
In Code – Poems

Will Cordeiro, *Trap Street (Able Muse Book Award for Poetry)*

John Philip Drury, *Sea Level Rising – Poems*

Rhina P. Espaillat, *And After All – Poems*

Anna M. Evans, *Under Dark Waters: Surviving the Titanic – Poems*

D. R. Goodman, *Greed: A Confession – Poems*

Carrie Green, *Studies of Familiar Birds – Poems*

Margaret Ann Griffiths, *Grasshopper – The Poetry of M A Griffiths*

Katie Hartsock, *Bed of Impatiens – Poems*

Elise Hempel, *Second Rain – Poems*

Jan D. Hodge, *Taking Shape – carmina figurata;*
The Bard & Scheherazade Keep Company – Poems

Ellen Kaufman, *House Music – Poems*
Double-Parked, with Tosca – Poems

Emily Leithauser, *The Borrowed World (Able Muse Book Award for Poetry)*

Hailey Leithauser, *Saint Worm – Poems*

Carol Light, *Heaven from Steam – Poems*

Kate Light, *Character Shoes – Poems*

April Lindner, *This Bed Our Bodies Shaped – Poems*

Martin McGovern, *Bad Fame – Poems*

Jeredith Merrin, *Cup – Poems*

Richard Moore, *Selected Poems;*
The Rule That Liberates: An Expanded Edition – Selected Essays

Richard Newman, *All the Wasted Beauty of the World – Poems*

Alfred Nicol, *Animal Psalms – Poems*

Deirdre O'Connor, *The Cupped Field (Able Muse Book Award for Poetry)*

Frank Osen, *Virtue, Big as Sin (Able Muse Book Award for Poetry)*

Alexander Pepple (Editor), *Able Muse Anthology;*
Able Muse – a review of poetry, prose & art (semiannual, winter 2010 on)

James Pollock, *Sailing to Babylon – Poems*

Aaron Poochigian, *The Cosmic Purr – Poems;*
Manhattanite (Able Muse Book Award for Poetry)

Tatiana Forero Puerta, *Cleaning the Ghost Room – Poems*

Jennifer Reeser, *Indigenous – Poems*

John Ridland, *Sir Gawain and the Green Knight (Anonymous) – Translation;*
Pearl (Anonymous) – Translation

Stephen Scaer, *Pumpkin Chucking – Poems*

Hollis Seamon, *Corporeality – Stories*

Ed Shacklee, *The Blind Loon: A Bestiary*

Carrie Shipers, *Cause for Concern (Able Muse Book Award for Poetry)*

Matthew Buckley Smith, *Dirge for an Imaginary World (Able Muse Book Award for Poetry)*

Susan de Sola, *Frozen Charlotte – Poems*

Barbara Ellen Sorensen, *Compositions of the Dead Playing Flutes – Poems*

Rebecca Starks, *Time Is Always Now – Poems;*
Fetch Muse – Poems

Sally Thomas, *Motherland – Poems*

J.C. Todd, *Beyond Repair – Poems*

Rosemerry Wahtola Trommer, *Naked for Tea – Poems*

Wendy Videlock, *Slingshots and Love Plums – Poems;*
The Dark Gnu and Other Poems;
Nevertheless – Poems

Richard Wakefield, *A Vertical Mile – Poems;*
Terminal Park – Poems

Gail White, *Asperity Street – Poems*

Chelsea Woodard, *Vellum – Poems*

Rob Wright, *Last Wishes – Poems*

www.ablemusepress.com

CPSIA information can be obtained
at www.ICGtesting.com
Printed in the USA
LVHW021211140920
665924LV00002B/127